A Year of Wicca: 52 Inspiring Essays on Wicca and Witchcraft

A Year of Wicca: 52 Inspiring Essays on Wicca and Witchcraft

Amethyst Treleven

Oak and Mistletoe

Oak and Mistletoe

PO Box 7393, Hutt Street, South Australia 5000, Australia

First Published 2009

A Year of Wicca: 52 Inspiring Essays on Wicca and Witchcraft © 2009
Amethyst Treleven

All rights reserved. No part of this publication may be reproduced, stored in a retrieval system, or transmitted, in any form or by any means, electronic, mechanical, photocopying, recording or otherwise, without the prior permission of the publisher in writing.

National Library of Australia Cataloguing-in-Publication entry

Author:	Treleven, Amethyst.
Title:	A year of Wicca : 52 inspiring essays on Wicca and witchcraft / Amethyst Treleven.
Edition:	1st ed.
ISBN:	9780980581843 (pbk.)
Subjects:	Wicca.
	Witchcraft.
Dewey Number:	133.43

For further information;

http://www.oakandmistletoe.com.au

For all my wonderful students. You teach me much more than I could ever teach you.

Table of Contents

3 simple ways to strengthen your magick 1
Can I cast a circle on the new moon? 3
Clairvoyance; what is it and do I want it? 6
Conducting rituals in public places 9
Crystals or crutch? 11
Lughnasadh/Lammas 13
How long does it take to learn Wicca? 18
How to shield yourself from psychic harm 20
Is a full moon esbat ritual really necessary? 23
Ritual is an outcome of Wicca as well as a practice of it 25
The difference between a handfasting and a marriage ceremony . 27
Autumn Equinox/Mabon 31
10 ways to determine the right coven for me 33
Are Wiccans the party faithful on polytheism? 37
'Being' Wiccan instead of 'doing' Wicca 39
Circle etiquette; what to do and not do in the circle 41
Cut the history lessons; just teach me the Wiccan juicy stuff! 44
Samhain/All Hallows 46
I'm a solitary; how do I get invited to a coven's festival? 49
How to dedicate yourself to the Wiccan deities 52
If finding Wicca is like going home, where's the floor plan? 55
Choosing a Craft or magickal name 57
Do you really need Wiccan ritual tools? 59
Learning about Wicca without being in a coven 61
Winter Solstice/Midwinter/Yule 63
Do I have to do Wiccan rituals naked? 65
Questions to ask a prospective Wiccan teacher 66
Setting up an altar at home 69
The dangers of being eclectic 71
What's the difference between divination and Wicca? 74
Imbolg/Candlemas 77
Negative and positive energy 82
Robes 84
Some of the best Wiccan and Witchcraft websites 86

The Book of Shadows and how to use it	88
Christian versus Wiccan ritual	92
The Wiccan obsession with 'stuff'	94
We don't just 'do' magick; we 'are' magick	99
Spring Equinox/Ostar/Eostre	101
Discrimination of non Christian faiths	104
3 steps to easy visualisation	106
Why I get up every morning	109
The differences in the southern and northern wheel of the year	111
Beltaine	114
Patron and matron deities	118
We learn Wicca and Witchcraft with our soul as well as our brain	120
Free access to Wiccan information and training	122
How covens are structured	125
Which books are great for newcomers to Wicca?	128
Wiccan magick meets "The Secret"	131
Summer Solstice/Midsummer's Eve/Litha	133
What does Christmas mean to a Wiccan?	136
What are your life values?	138

Acknowledgements

I have been blessed so much and with every day that passes my amazement and awe continues. The Goddess delivers to me daily the blessing of a loving family, a spiritual community that gives me as much as I give it and a life I am truly grateful for.

To all my loved ones, thank you for your ongoing support, encouragement and love. I am sincerely grateful.

With smiles and blessings,

Amethyst

1ˢᵗ January

3 simple ways to strengthen your magick

Magick is beautiful and something I not only have immense respect for but also use in one way or another almost every day. So with universality in mind, I thought I'd pass on these three simple tips I've developed over the years which help me significantly strengthen the magick I perform each and every day.

For me, magick is a way of harnessing my own inner energies and also focusing those of the universe around me to bring about a specified outcome. The key is having the specified outcome though in the first place. If you don't have a very clear, very well defined and easily articulated outcome, how on earth will the universe know exactly what you want? It's a bit like saying that you want to take a drive; but where to? If you don't know where you're going, how will you know when you've arrived? Similarly if you can't really describe exactly what you want from your magick, then how will the universe know what to get for you?

Tip 1
Before you start, really make sure you have absolutely clearly defined your expected outcome. For me the easiest way to do that is to write it down. Even dot points will help:

- What exactly are you expecting?
- What colour is it?
- When will it happen?
- What date?
- What size is it?
- What model is it?
- What does it look like?
- What does it feel like?
- What exact impact does it have on your life?

The dot points are obviously determined by what the magick is about but essentially the key here is to be absolutely specific.

Tip 2
Write those dot points down and stick them to your bathroom mirror or somewhere similar where you'll see them every day. Magick comes about as a result of focused thought, concentrated energy and that focus, that concentration, that repeated and continued referral to your desired outcome makes the magick that much more potent. Depending on what it is you're doing the magick for, you may need that note up there for a day or so, a few days, several weeks even. If for example you've decided to use magick to help you lose weight then you may need that note up there for a few weeks or even months to keep you tightly blinkered to your weight goal and to keep the magick clearly focused on that outcome. The more you see that outcome in front of you, the more the universe knows how important it is and this magnifies the effort to bring it about.

Tip 3
Double check again why you want your magickal outcome. This is probably the most important step you'll ever use in magick and if you never do anything else, please do this. Ask yourself again why do you want this particular outcome? Why do you want to lose weight? Is it because you want to be healthier? Then OK, but perhaps then you should also be asking for better health. Is it because you want to feel happier about yourself? There's nothing wrong with that at all, but perhaps that's what you should actually be asking for. What I'm saying here is that sometimes we get caught up in doing magick to bring about the easy bandaid solutions rather than addressing the real and often harder underlying issue. If all we ever do is try and solve something with bandaid solutions, we'll soon run out of bandaids, the wound will remain and what's more, may gradually become infected.

8th January

Can I cast a circle on the new moon?

It's quite true that many Wiccans conduct their main esbats on the full moon but many also celebrate the new or dark moon with as much celebration and joy. The question for new students is often "why?" Let's look at the differences between the full and new moon so we can see why the new moon can be as important as the full moon.

When the moon is full, her energy is at its height and of course the pull and strength of the moon is reflected in the tides around the globe. There's even more evidence that a full moon signals the time of the strongest, global energy. Statistics clearly show that more murders, violence and unusual events occur during the full moon part of the lunar cycle than at any other time. If you couple that with unusual heat or humidity then suicides, crime, episodes of insanity and unruly behaviour skyrocket. The police force, welfare agencies and support services like Centrelink (Australia's Social Security) know and prepare for this cyclic rise in events. Many years ago I used to work for Social Security and staff would always know that there were more incidents around the full moon period than at any other time of the lunar cycle.

So what does this tell us? It highlights that the moon has a direct influence over our behaviour and over the strength of our magick. Conducting magick at the full moon injects just that little more power into it and is a perfect time for doing 'diminishing' types of magick. Diminishing magick is spell-craft that makes something go away, get smaller or reduce. Banishing magick is a great example of that. If you want to give up smoking, then that's an example also of diminishing magick. You want your cravings for cigarettes to diminish for example. So when we want something to go away, or get smaller, if we do it when the moon will also be getting smaller, we'll be doing the magick in tune with the natural forces of the lunar cycle.

The new moon by contrast is the time when the lunar energy level is at rest and is about to slowly and gently climb again. As such it's a great time to do 'expanding' magick. As the moon and its energy expands, so too can your magick and its results. Expanding magick is spell-craft conducted to create something or to increase something. For example you might want to increase your self esteem of bring more love into your life. The new moon is a great opportunity to match your need for more of something at a time when there will also be more and more of the moon and her powerful energy to bring to your spell-craft.

For many covens, the new moon becomes the night for training, either for Outer Court students but often for those more advanced and initiated members looking to improve their skills and work towards higher degrees. Given the lower energy levels of the lunar cycle, it forces the magickal practitioner to work harder, to test themselves more strongly and devise more intense means of creating and directing magickal energies. Thus it's a fabulous time to really push skills towards more advanced levels of competency.

With the light of the new moon so limited as well, covens and solitaries are much more likely to work outdoors perhaps in forests or by the ocean because it's less likely that outsiders can spot them and watch what they do. With such bright light at the full moon, it's easier to be spotted than it is when the moon's light is dim and softer or virtually nonexistent.

Finally, and probably most importantly, is that it actually doesn't matter when you conduct your circle casting. The main reason for casting a circle is to honour the Lord and Lady and you actually don't need a moon to do that. She's a wonderful symbol of the feminine aspect of the universe's Divine, but you can still honour and respect deity regardless of whether the moon is full or dark, whether it's hidden in clouds or extenuated by the smoke of a harvest bonfire. Many covens don't adhere to a schedule of full and new moon cycles at all, but instead meet on the first Saturday of each month because it's easier to get everyone together on a Saturday than on a Tuesday work night when the moon might be full. Still other covens, and solitaires in particular, will just cast a circle and honour the Divine when the feeling takes them regardless of the date or the passage of the moon. Whilst it's nice to use the splendour and delight of the full moon to aid your circles of worship, your prime objective should always be to love our Lord and Lady and you can do that anytime.

15th January

Clairvoyance; what is it and do I want it?

Did you know that over the last 20 years at least one third of people in the USA believe in clairvoyance[1]? This is really amazing when many folk don't actually realize that there is also clairaudience, clairsentience, clairalience, claircognizance and clairgustance. But let's focus on clairvoyance first before we get too carried away.

Clairvoyance comes from the French language spoken during the 1600's and means clear (clair) and visibility (voyance). In other words, if someone is a clairvoyant, they have an ability for clear sight that others may not have. In our current lifetime, clairvoyance is much more associated with people who are generally able to gain information or an understanding about people, events or activities that might not normally be available through usual channels. Genuine clairvoyants the world over have an innate but trained skill that enables them to tap into a wisdom and knowledge source many people don't have the same keys for. Technically speaking, folk who have clairvoyant skills can see, literally, pictures and scenes of events and people and places in the future, in the past and across different continents.

They have an ability to reach into portals and view different life movies that most people simply can't register.

Clairaudience by contrast refers to that skill whereby people can hear information about people or events or places. They report that the sounds are either 'in their head' or all around them and in listening they're able to connect with untapped wisdom and provide that to others.

Clairsentience is the ability to feel or touch and receive otherwise unknown information. More usually clairsentients feel a sensation like cold or warmth, or the touch of a spiritual hand, or the feel of the spray of the ocean or another event that provides information and wisdom. They're then able to interpret that and understand the messages provided.

Then we have clairalience which is the more unusual skill of receiving information through aromas and smells and scents. A practitioner may be able to smell the lavender that Great Aunt Josephine used to wear, or perhaps they can smell the scent of newly mown grass. Maybe they can smell the famous cakes that their neighbour used to bake before they passed on, or perhaps smell the hospital room that their friend or client Susan passed over in. Aromatherapy tells us that smells are powerful tools for changing our moods but they also bring back old memories or generate new ones for the practitioner smelling the relevant aromas of their client.

Claircognizance is a skill many of us have but that we mistake for the more general term of clairvoyance. To be claircogizant is to 'know'. How often has something happened to you and you 'just know' that it's your Mum on the phone before you answer it, or that your friend needs your help, or that one of the kids is unwell even though their 50 miles away. That's claircognizance. Probably one of the most prevalent forms of this skill set and yet almost always mislabelled.

Finally clairgustance is the much more rare skill of gaining information, wisdom and insight from taste. Very often we remember special events by familiar and well loved tastes. When you indulge on that gorgeous trifle, does it not remind you of Sunday family lunches when Mum used to always make trifle? Remember how you used to poke your tongue at your brother at the table while Dad wasn't looking and how he used to kick your shins under the table? That's clairgustance when you can taste the foods of other people's events that perhaps you were never present at.

But would you want one or more of these gifts? Most of us actually do have one or more but we've lost the use of them and if we wanted to rekindle them, we'd need training in them. The key is to be able to use the gifts 'on demand' rather than have them thrown at you at the whim of the spirit and universal world. They can be destructive when not controlled and thus that training is very important. That's usually part of your second and subsequent degree studies in Wicca although you can find local specialists who can help you develop those skills outside the religious framework. Just trust your instincts when choosing a teacher and then enjoy the sensations of your extra perceptions.

[1] Carrol, Robert (2003), "Clairvoyance" - *Skeptics Dictionary*. http://www.skepdic.com/clairvoy.html accessed 2nd February 2009.

22nd January

Conducting rituals in public places

It's often wonderful to get a group of people together (or even for the solitary) to conduct a ritual or two in a beautiful public area like a forest, the beach or even the local park. Sabbats in particular a wonderful occasions to get out and about and share the ritual with friends and loved ones at a park close to everyone or a peaceful patch of farmland or whatever. There's something very special about honouring deity with friends and loved ones amidst the splendour of the mountains, trees, grasslands or the sea. However, to make sure that the occasion goes well, and that there are no legal, journalistic or embarrassing consequences afterwards, the following tips might prove very helpful.

- To avoid curious stares or visitors, don't wear ritual robes or elaborate clothing unless the place is very private.
- However, do wear clothing to avoid police intervention and charges of nudity!
- Always leave the area cleaner than you found it.
- If the area is run by a municipality or similar, seek permission to use the area first.

- If you are allowed to light a fire, keep a hose, water bucket or safety materials close by.
- Keep the noise down.
- If erecting equipment like a maypole or similar, make sure this does not damage the area.
- Be aware that any loud, supposedly socially unusual behaviour or singing will attract attention.
- Dancing around a circle area may well attract onlookers so either keep dancing to a minim or choose a very private area.
- Rituals done during the evening and night will often need candles. Be aware of fire bans and safety or use battery lanterns instead.

Essentially your aim with a ritual in a public place rather than at home is to conduct the rite with respect for not only deity, but also for the owners and users of the area in question. You wouldn't want people coming in and leaving scorch marks on your lawn from a ritual fire or leaving their lolly wrappers and empty drink cartons all over your neatly weeded flowerbeds! If you wouldn't be happy with that at your place, neither would anyone else at a public place either.

29th January

Crystals or crutch?

OK, I know this will be controversial but I was never one to shy away from a discussion! I had a thought this week which concerned me. Anyone who knows me will know that I love my crystals (amethyst ,what a surprise, and clear quartz particularly) and that I usually carry some crystals with me. I'll often have a small smooth crystal or two shoved discreetly down my bra (a lot more comfortable than t sounds) and I often carry a drawstring pouch with my favourite crystals nestled within it. The pouch hangs off my shoulder even at work.

Why do I do this? Because it feels comforting, because I like to draw strength from them when things get tough particularly at work and because I can. I find that holding a crystal when I'm feeling a little stressed, perplexed, worried or frustrated helps me focus and can keep me calm. All great stuff I reckon until I wondered if my crystals had become a crutch rather than simply a tool to refocus my inner strengths. I really questioned myself here and searched my motivation and reasons for using my crystals. Had I become so dependent on them that they had replaced my own strengths? Horror! Was I actually a 'cyrstalholic'? Did I have a crystal dependency problem? Was I a crystal addict?

Seriously now, and no offence intended to anyone (heaven knows in reality my very real addiction is chocolate – just ask my partner!) I came to the conclusion that my crystals were still a tool rather than a crutch. I realised that I could live my life quite easily without them and in fact I don't have them with me every day, most days admittedly but not every day.

The more I thought it through, the more I realised that we all use a variety of objects, rituals, habits and behaviours to help us steer through life's challenges. One of my best friends is clearly addicted to coffee and that's something she absolutely needs in order to get going each morning. My partner loves reading the paper on a Sunday morning and apart from that having become his Sunday morning ritual, it's something he frets for if it doesn't happen. I bet we all have behaviours or little objects we use regularly that have become our ritualised ways of coping or at least support mechanisms. But having said that, most of us still have enough inner strength to cope even when our much loved object or behaviour is missing. I love my crystals but I also equally have enough self strength to get through life without a crutch if I have to, well maybe with the exception of chocolate.

5th February

Lughnasadh/Lammas

A Greater Sabbat and an Earth Cross-Quarter Day
Northern Hemisphere July 31st
Southern Hemisphere February 2nd
Seasonal Relevancy
Some of the flowers are already beginning to fade while the late bloomers are coming into their fullness. The new life that came in spring is fast developing toward adulthood and we're beginning to see the outcomes of the fertile energies sewn earlier in the seasonal cycle and year.

This festival celebrates the first harvest being brought in from the fields and from the fruit trees and so rituals tend to focus on the theme of harvest.

Mythological Relevancy
Lughnasadh (pronounced 'Loo-nar-sar) is a ritual often held in honour of the ancient Celtic sun God Lugh and it marks how he annually sacrifices his life so that the fruits can ripen and the crops can grow toward their harvests. Lugh is a revered God of harvest and light.

Popular Rituals
Bake bread from many different grains to honour the harvest and celebrate the food of the Gods.

A Contemporary Lughnasadh/Lammas Ritual

Everyone should begin gathering at the ritual site late in the afternoon so that the ritual can commence close to sunset. The circle is to be marked out with a trail of grain. The altar is to be decorated with the flowers that are currently in season (Iris, Lilies, Frangipani, Lavender, Jasmine etc) and with the bread rolls that each person has been asked to bring with them. Cakes and ale should be small bread rolls and red wine. Each person is to bring with them their ingredients for summer pudding (see below).

Cast the circle as normal if there are no visitors present, otherwise, omit the circle casting.

The ritual leader commences by explaining Lammas "Lammas is an ancient Celtic fire festival that celebrates the first grain harvest of the season and also marks the turning point between summer and the commencement of autumn. In times gone by, people would have used this opportunity to give thanks for the bounty of the harvest and to begin the preparations for the coming dark, winter months. Winter was a harsh time when many animals and people did not survive either because of the cold, through hunger or through illness. The harvest was therefore extremely important because the grain helped ensure adequate supplies of food through those coming months".

"Lammas comes from the Anglo Saxon word, hlafmas or loaf-mass and shows us that a thousand years ago, the grain crops were of immense importance to the ongoing survival of village life. Many cultures across the globe celebrate a similar concept at this time. The Irish honour the solar God Lugh with their Lughnasadh festival. Lugh was the king of the Tuatha de Danann, the God of light and of the harvest and this festival marks the point at which he begins to die in sacrifice to ensure an abundant crop. The Scots call this event Lunasduinn, the French honour the God Lugus while even the Christians adopted this festival to celebrate St Peter's release from prison."

"As a celebration of the grain harvest that delivers increased opportunity to survive the coming months, bread is the icon of Lammas. Bread is the product of the grain and thus the embodiment of continued life. Christians see bread as the body of Christ while Greek mythology sees bread as a symbol of mortality. Bread, like wine, is a food substance that undergoes a fermentation process and as such bread, and wine, are separated from the usual fruits of the harvest which need little preparation before consumption. Apples, oranges, nuts, berries, vegetables and many other fruits of the land can be eaten almost straight from the tree, the vine, the bush or the ground. They may require washing or even simple cooking but grain and grapes undergo a process of modification in order to become the revered produce they are and this process symbolises civilisation, community and the intellectualisation of man."

"Bread is thus the symbol of life, of man's ability to survive but also of the separation between the immortal world of the Gods and the mundane and harsh world of mortal man."

"As we celebrate this festival, let us each consider what we have to be grateful for today. What are the things you are reaping now that you began last year? What are the bounties that you are grateful for? What are the blessings that have enriched your life? Moreover, what are the things you need to do now in order to prepare for the darkness of winter? What are the things you must think about that will bring you happiness and peace during the next six months? What processes do you need to start right now that will help you reach your goals?"

At this point each person present is given a bread roll from those that were placed on the altar prior to the commencement of the ritual.

The ritual leader says "each of you has brought to this rite some bread which is a symbol of enduring life. The bread you hold in your hand is like the bread that came from the grain harvests which enabled our ancestors to live through the extremes of winter. The Irish-Gaelic God Lugh gave his life for the harvest so that the cycle of life could continue. Break your bread in half now and before you take a bite, consider the bounty that you have for which you can be grateful. If you would like, please share your thoughts of thanks."

Each person can then share what they are grateful for with the group and take a bite of their bread roll.

The ritual leader now continues "while each of us has issues of concern and problems that we face, the likelihood that we will die from starvation or cold through the winter is not strong. We are blessed to be part of a community that has bread, that has heating, supermarkets, jobs, money, transport. It may not always be a bed of roses, but we are blessed more than many others. Take one more bite of your bread and as you do, give thoughts to those who do not share in your blessings."

Each person can take one more bite in silent contemplation.

The ritual leader completes this ritual task by asking the group to place their left over bread pieces back in the altar bowl and explains that these left over pieces will go to feed the local chickens and birds so contributing to the continued cycle of life.

Consecrate and then have the cakes and ale then close the circle. Follow up by making summer puddings together.

The ritual leader says "while grains are abundant now, so too are berries. The supermarkets are awash with blueberries, mulberries, blackberries, strawberries and so on. The season is brief and the fruits are so yummy that it would be a shame not to incorporate these into our Lughnasadh/Lammas event. So each person is going to make a summer pudding using the berries, bread and bowls they brought with them. (To help with this, a recipe is included below.)

The ritual leader explains how to make the pudding and why it is significant "the berries are abundant now but the season will be over within the month. The redcurrants, strawberries, raspberries and so on are the colour of dark fire, the colour of the fire Gods, the colour of blood which is the universal liquid of life. The bread that surrounds the berries within the pudding bowl incorporates the bread aspect of this festival and envelops the berry red blood of life within a symbolic bread shell of enduring life. The summer pudding is thus our symbol of survival."

"Once made, the pudding will then chill in the fridge overnight so that it becomes solid and edible and this storage reflects how the grain of our ancestors was stored to be consumed later. Our summer pudding is thus a tribute to our past and a way to connect with the fruits of our harvest."

This should be a joyous and fun filled occasion given the abundance of life around us and the promise of enough food through so as everyone makes the summer puddings, they can sing along with the old Celtic folksongs that so often told the stories of these times.

Summer Pudding Recipe[1]
Serves 6
- 8 oz (225 g) redcurrants
- 4 oz (110 g) blackcurrants
- 1lb (450 g) raspberries
- 5oz (150 g) castor sugar
- 7-8 medium slices white bread from a large loaf
- You will also need a 1½ pint (850 ml) pudding basin, lightly buttered.

Separate the redcurrants and blackcurrants from their stalks by holding the tip of each stalk firmly between finger and thumb and sliding it between the prongs of a fork pushing the fork downwards, so pulling off the berries as it goes. Rinse all the fruits, picking out any raspberries that look at all musty. Using the very freshest, unmarked fruits will ensure a much tastier and appealing pudding.

Place the fruits with the sugar in a large saucepan over a medium heat and let them gently cook for about 3-5 minutes, only until the sugar has dissolved and the juices begin to run – don't overcook and so spoil the fresh flavour. Once cooked, now remove the fruit from the heat, and line the pudding basin with the slices of bread, overlapping them and sealing well by pressing the edges of the slices together. Fill in any gaps with small pieces of bread, so that no juice can get through when you add the fruit.

Pour the fruit and juice in (except for about two thirds of a cupful which will be used later), then cover the pudding with another slice of bread. Then place a small plate or saucer (one that will fit exactly inside the rim of the bowl) on top, and on top of that place a 3 lb or 4 lb (1.3 kg or 1.8 kg) weight, and leave in the fridge overnight. This ensures the pudding is compressed and soaks up the fruit juice.

Just before serving the pudding, turn it out on to a large serving dish and spoon the reserved juice all over it, to soak into any bits of bread that still appear to look white. Serve the pudding, cut into wedges, along with a bowl of whipped, thickened cream on the table. Leftovers can be refrigerated for later use and these will keep several days if stored appropriately.

[1]http://www.deliaonline.com/recipes/type-of-dish/summer-desserts/summer-pudding.html accessed 4th July 2009.

12th February

How long does it take to learn Wicca?

The simple answer I normally give to this question is "a lifetime" but I figure that's probably not going to be enough words for an InfoCircle edition, so let's explore why it takes a lifetime.

Let's get something clear here. Learning Wicca isn't as simple as learning how to bake the chocolate cake in that cookery book or even learning how to drive in order to pass your test. You don't learn to 'do' Wicca, you learn to 'become' Wiccan, there's a distinct difference. When you learn how to bake that chocolate cake you don't become a 'chocolate cake baker' necessarily. It doesn't usually become something that defines your beliefs and your way of life. Similarly passing your driving test might be a huge achievement and may give you lots more freedom to get around legally but it doesn't change who you are.

Wicca, the religious belief system and it's practices, takes a lifetime to learn because you're constantly learning who you are. We never get to the point when we know ourselves completely. The study of Wicca is thus a lifetime commitment to continuing that exploration; that expose and that commitment to make ourselves a better, more holistic person.

One of the frustrations of so many Wiccan teachers is that some students want to learn everything this week and become Third Degree experts by next month. Just because you can cast a circle, maybe work a spell or two, have a better understanding of nature and your place within it than you did last year, doesn't mean you know it all. There's no pinnacle with Wicca, there's no end result, there's no prize label that describes you as Wicca's ultimate authority. You just continue with life's Wiccan journey till you die which means everyday you learn new ways to 'be' Wiccan as well as to 'do' Wicca.

Let's get practical though just to appease the critics and I'll give you some general time frames around traditional learning processes. In preparation for initiation, students will often take at least a year and a day although with the Inclusive tradition, our training program takes eight months. Once initiated, the practitioner then spends between one and two years working towards their Second Degree initiation although having said that, many Wiccans are happy to remain as First Degrees thereafter. Once at Second Degree, the practitioner can take anything up to ten years before they're initiated to Third Degree. So within the more traditional timeframes, you can be practising for almost fifteen years before you lead your own coven.

Having said that, even then you're still learning. You still come across new events new students and new situations every day that challenge and build on what you already know, or think you know! Most practitioners will create new sabbat rituals every year so that means new learnings every year with each ritual. Most covens, and even solitaires, change the way they do things from time to time and that s all new learning too.

So learning about Wicca doesn't have a fixed timeframe because you're not just learning a skill set, you're learning about you and your place in our wonderful, spiritual universe. Given that the person you think you know today will be slightly different tomorrow, you'll be learning new things about yourself tomorrow, and the day after, and the day after that and the day after that too. Becoming Wiccan is therefore a lifelong commitment, so how long does it take to learn Wicca? Well now you know the answer!

19th Feb

How to shield yourself from psychic harm

One of the things that new students often ask me is how to protect themselves from the negative energies of others around them. As an example, just this morning one of my work colleagues (who is also a massage therapist and has a real empathy with energy movements) asked how she could best emotionally protect herself from a domineering, unsympathetic and belligerent boss. Psychic protection is often similar to, and connected with, emotional protection. If you feel good then you're in a better position to attract positive rather than negative energies. Furthermore, when you feel sad, upset, angry or frightened, you're much more likely to attract negative energies and have the anger and frustrations of others 'stick to you'. So what do you do about that?

Well, there's two really easy ways to help protect yourself from someone else's sludgy energies or even from the really nasty stuff like other people's tempers and tantrums or simply dark forces that make you feel very uncomfortable. The first, and softer approach, is the egg shell protection and like the second protection method is really easy to do.

Egg Shell Protection

You might think of egg shells being very delicate and quite easily broken, well not this one! Make sure you've drawn into yourself all the white light and pure energy that you need using your normal method. (This may be from the earth below you or from breathing in pure, clean energy with each in-breath.) Make sure you've cleansed your aura so that you're brimming with white light and that your aura is clean, fresh and sparkling.

Now imagine yourself cocooned inside an egg. See the egg shell surrounding you with both you and your aura safely tucked up comfortably inside it. Feel the pure softness of the yellow yolk flowing through and around you and bathe in the protection and comfort of the clear egg white. You're being nurtured within the safety and womb of the egg.

Now imagine that the shell of the egg is made of Kevlar, and while it's light and fine, its strength is so immense that it could stop a bullet. Nothing can get through it unless you let it. You look closer and see that your Kevlar shell is actually made of a sieve like structure with tiny one millimetre holes all the way through it. The holes have been designed to let through only good, positive energy so that you can stream white energy and love to others and they can stream it back to you because that wonderful clean, fresh and pure energy can fit easily through those tiny holes. However, and here's the true strength of your egg shell protection, the holes are too small to let through the bigger particles of negative, dark and unwanted energies.

So when that impatient boss, or the nasty neighbour or the darker energy force comes crashing toward you, its energy simply can't penetrate your Kevlar egg shell. The holes that let through good energies are too small to let through anything unwanted! You're protected, your safe and you're still bathing and luxuriating in the comfort and love of your egg yolk.

The Mirror Ball

When you need an instant and much more hard-hitting protection mechanism, the mirror ball is a great way to go. With practice, you can get this one up instantly whenever you might need it. It's great to be able to have the time to bring white light into yourself and cleanse your aura but usually when you need the mirror ball, there isn't enough time to do those preliminaries.

So whenever you're faced with some real anger, even danger and some frightening people, events or energies, see yourself cradled inside a mirror ball. Make sure it completely surrounds you and that it's clean and bright and shiny. Nothing can get through your mirror ball at all regardless of good or bad. It is completely solid and strong and rigid.

Notice that it reflects everything around it and energy and emotions from others may head towards the mirror ball but as soon as they hit it, no matter where they come from, those nasty emotions, that anger, that dark and frightening behaviour just bounces right back to the source. The mirror ball is exactly that, a mirror that reflects everything that comes towards it. All the bad stuff someone throws at you bounces straight back at them while you remain safe and warm and comfortable cocooned within the safety of the mirror ball. What this also means is that whoever or whatever aims some darker words or behaviours your way simply cops their own sludge straight back again psychically just as the law of return suggests. What's even more fantastic though is that if anyone sends some good energies your way, that bounces back and makes them feel good too!

Make sure to practice both these protection strategies so that you can generate the shields when you need them. They can be invaluable at work, at home, socially and in the circle.

26th Feb

Is a full moon esbat ritual really necessary?

In conversations with students, and indeed with many longer term Wiccans as well, it seems to me that full moon esbat rituals have become the accepted necessity, the expected norm if you like and this worries me. If you look at the evidential history of Wicca, in the beginning under Gerald Gardner rituals were rarely conducted at full moons and instead it was the sabbats that were the main focus of group ritual. In truth, the full moon esbats we tend to conduct now came about in later years. That's OK, but I guess what worries me is the potential issue of conducting an esbat because it's expected rather than because it's wanted.

For many people in more mainstream religions, one of the frequent complaints is that their regular Sunday or Sabbath services, sermons and rituals have become routine. For example, many Christians are expected to attend Sunday services because "that's what you do" as I was once told. Isn't it a bit sad when you 'have to' attend a service because that's what's expected on that day at that time? Wouldn't the Gods and Goddesses prefer to see us honour them because we want to and because it feels right rather than because that day or date has come around?

Let me make it clear that I'm not suggesting we all shun full moon esbats. I'm certainly not saying that we shouldn't conduct these wonderful rites. I love my full moon rite and I know the coven members love getting together as a community to share their love of deity and to honour their fellowship with one another. What I am suggesting however is that if those rites end up being conducted because that's what you 'have to do' rather than that's what you'd like to do, then they've become an institutionalised expectation rather than a rite of honour and love.

If I feel like casting a circle and honouring the Divine, then I do that. I do it on a full moon because I like to, but I'll often do it say on a Tuesday, or maybe a Friday. I'll do it at 11am, maybe at 8:30pm, maybe I'll do it because it's raining, maybe because I want to say thanks for my daughter's smiles, maybe because a God or Goddess is calling me or because the washing machine is fixed now, or maybe because I just feel like it. If any of that falls on a full moon, then great and if it doesn't, then so what?

In other words, I wonder if it's dangerous to always timetable the ritual. full moon esbats are wonderful but so are spontaneous rituals for whatever reason is right at the time. The Gods and Goddesses should be honoured all the time and any time, not just because the calendar says so.

5th March

Ritual is an outcome of Wicca as well as a practice of it

Anthropology and Sociology have traditionally defined ritual (including Wiccan ritual) as a function of religion and a function of society. Hmmm... All very well and good until we look a little further at ritual and its purpose and see the context in which Wiccans actually use it.

For many religions, especially the more mainstream and traditional ones, the rituals they use serve to supposedly bring their parishioners closer to their deity. The rituals become a fait accompli, a sort of expectation of communal reverence. Everyone crowds into the church, temple, synagogue or whatever, follow the ritual conducted by the priest/minister/father and hope like heck they paid their dues to their God. In other words, it may not have taught them much about life or themselves or even their God but it served the purpose of going to church and doing the right thing.

Religions and faith systems that lay more responsibility on the practitioner for ritual design like Wicca serve a broader purpose than that. Not only are they ways to connect with the Gods and Goddesses but they're also learning events and the result of learning. As students of Wicca, you will usually be asked to contribute to and eventually design your own rituals, especially for sabbats. For students learning within a group, you'll be coached in how to write and conduct a ritual for maximum effect and for solitary learners, you'll probably be learning by following suggestions in a book or even by trial and error. So ritual becomes not just a way to honour the Divine, but also a way to learn how to honour the Divine.

Then once you've written a few rituals, conducted a few and designed different ways to morph your rituals into personalised events of honour, you will have reached a stage where those same rituals are the outcome of your learning to be Wiccan. So now ritual is a way to honour the Divine, a methodology for learning and a result of your learning. Compare that to parishioners who just go to church on a Sunday and follow what is presented to them!

So being a Wiccan and a Witch is also a wonderful way to take control of your own learning, to take control of the rituals you use to honour the Divine and to measure how far you've come in your training. Clever us Wiccans eh?!

12th March

The difference between a handfasting and a marriage ceremony

I'm often asked about the difference between these two celebrations and there definitely seems to be some confusion between the content and indeed intent of the two. So let's play at being dictionaries first and make sure we have our definitions clearly defined.

A handfasting ritual is essentially a spiritual promise before the Gods and Goddesses to partner together for a period of time, for the rest of this mortal life or even for eternity. A marriage ceremony by contrast, is ultimately a legal declaration but can also be a religious commitment to remain together as man and wife (or a same sex marriage in some parts of the world) for the rest of this mortal life. Just to complicate matters though, a handfasting can also be a legal marriage ceremony as well. Confused yet?

Let's explore the marriage ceremony first because that's the easier of the two concepts to really comprehend. Legal marriage, at least here in Australia, is the "union of a man and woman, to the exclusion of all others, for life" as defined by the Marriage Act and Regulations 1961. The ceremony must be solemnised by either a registered minister of a recognised church denomination or by a legally registered civil celebrant. Legal weddings can also be conducted by other persons under certain circumstances such as for certain couples outside Australian waters like service personal and so on. However, for the most part, only those two recognised types of persons can solemnise a legal wedding celebration.

That's not to say that someone else can't conduct a great deal or even the majority of the ceremony. Many weddings, particularly civil ones can, and do, include all sorts of small rituals and traditions and these can really turn an otherwise 'standardised' ceremony into something more personal and unique. In order for the ceremony to be recognised and to result in a registered marriage, the civil celebrant or minister must briefly talk through and say three different sets of wordings. These word sets can be modified but their meaning can't be changed or modified. Essentially the celebrant or minister must discuss what marriage actually means, they must ask the couple if they intend to marry and be party to the vows, and they must declare them as husband and wife. In addition, they also have to produce three copies of a marriage certificate, lodge them with the relevant state authority and so on but what all this means is that as long as the officiating person includes those words and does those actions, the rest of the ceremony can be absolutely designed by the couple.

At the conclusion, the couple (who must be a man and woman in Australia) are legally coupled together, are legally obliged to support one another and can only escape from their bonds via divorce, annulment or where the ceremony was conducted illegally. Essentially then it's a legally binding contract to partner with one another for life and while a religious ceremony may also be conducted before the deity of that recognised religion (primarily Christian in Australia), the ceremony itself remains a legal and lawful contract.

Handfasting by contrast need have no legal basis to it and is purely a promise of partnership before the Gods and Goddesses or the patron and matron deities of the couple in question. However, where all the legal's are included and it's conducted by a registered civil celebrant (or minister of a church although a Pagan handfasting is unlikely to be conducted within a Christian or more traditional faith form), it can also become a legally binding contract of marriage.

Without those legal inclusions however, and within the essential meaning of handfasting, the ceremony can be conducted for a same sex or heterosexual couple, and it can also be conducted as either a 'wedding' with a full commitment or as an 'engagement' and promise to marry later. In fact it can also be conducted well after a couple originally married or handfasted as a means of renewing and affirming their original vows.

The handfasting can also have a timeframe placed on it as well. Unlike a legal marriage in Australia which is "for life" as defined by the Marriage Act, you can handfast with your partner for the common time frame of a year and a day. At the end of that period you can either elect to recommit with another handfasting or walk away.

Couples can however handfast with one another for the term of their mortal life which is similar to the legal marriage requirement and some couples have even promised to remain together into future lives as well. Essentially the timeframe for the life of a handfasting is up to the couple and contrasts with its legal counterpart. The legal marriage vow expects the couple to commit "until death us do part" or similar wording, while the more flexible handfasting traditionally states that the couple will be together "for as long as the love shall last".

There's an important note to consider here worthy of attention. Some critics of the handfasting will suggest that if you only commit "for as long as the love shall last" then it's an easy licence to walk away from your spouse after you have a tiff over who left the toilet seat up or down. The truth is that the handfasting is a pledge and a commitment before the Divine, to partner together for that period and that's what your expected to do. It's not a marriage licence free from a breakfast cereal packet and it's not something you can simply discard again because you've changed your mind. When you commit to a partnership, you do exactly that, you commit. So just because you don't have that legal document saying you're bound together, you are in fact bound by a much stronger force, your pledge and promise to the Lord and Lady. In other words, a handfasting is a religious ceremony of promise declared before the Divine and is more binding spiritually than any legal piece of paper.

So while it's a spiritual promise, the handfasting can be conducted by anyone the couple feels comfortable with. Many couples handfast themselves while others ask their High Priestess or a trusted spiritual advisor or friend to witness their promises before the Gods and Goddesses. However, remember that if they also want the handfasting to be legally binding, then a civil celebrant or church minister must conduct the legally required sections of the ceremony and then it becomes a merging of a handfasting and a legal marriage ceremony.

A handfasting is often much less expensive than a traditional legal ceremony because the couple often see that the commitment itself is more important than the pomp and ceremony usually accompanying the traditional big white wedding. The bride and groom are sometimes naked but more frequently they both wear simple clothes and often have no attendants. There's usually feasting afterwards but it's usually simple and the celebration is often conducted in a forest or near a stream or the ocean, or in fact anywhere where the couple feel especially close to deity. Where the couple have Christian families or others who may not understand or appreciate the concept of a handfasting, the couple may opt to have a handfasting to honour their love of the Lord and Lady but also follow that with a legal wedding to appease the family.

So there you have it, the marriage ceremony versus the handfasting ritual. Quite different from one another in many respects and with often completely different intents and purposes but they're two ritual celebrations which can also be combined into one or done separately. Confusing really eh?!

19th March

Autumn Equinox/Mabon

A Lesser Sabbat and a Sun Quarter Day
Northern Hemisphere September 21st
Southern Hemisphere March 21st
Seasonal Relevancy
At this time of year, there's an equal balance of light and dark, summer and winter, male and female. The second grain harvest is brought in, the fruits are ready and the animal hunt begins to ramp back up.

Mythological Relevancy
There's equilibrium between male and female energies again so this festival honours the balance between good and bad, light and dark, male and female. It is a time of universal balance across all spiritual and physical elements.

Popular Traditions
Save some ears of corn or grain from the harvest to make into a Brigid's Cross at Imbolg. Keep the corn or grain ears safe and dry within your home ready for use.

A Contemporary Autumn Equinox - Mabon Ritual
The altar should be decorated with different fruits and vegetables. There should be a basket of apples with one apple

for every two people present and a knife. An empty cauldron sits in the circle centre.

Cast the circle as normal if there are no visitors present, otherwise, omit the circle casting.

The High Priestess opens the ritual saying "the autumn equinox signals the midpoint in the journey of the sun across the seasons. As we celebrate this day, let us remember that there is balance in all things, day and night, light and dark, life and death, good fortune and misfortune. Let this rite be one of honour for the balance in seasons and in life."

The maiden takes the basket of apples from before the altar and cuts them in half across its middle saying "the apple is a sacred fruit and contains the five pointed star. The points of the star herein mark the balance of the elements Air, Fire, Water, Earth and Spirit in all things." She hands a half apple to the first covener saying "blessed and thankful are we for the balance of our lives". The covener replies "blessed be." She repeats this for each covener until everyone has an apple.

The High Priest says "each of you have one half of a whole. For balance to continue there must always be a joining of dark and light, good and bad for nothing sits alone."

The High Priest and High Priestess come together and press the two halves of their apples together. She says "we come together in harmony and balance as the Lord and Lady come together through the seasons." Together they raise their apple pressed together to the sky and the High Priest says "may we give thanks for the balance of the Lord and Lady above and for the balance in our lives below".

The maiden asks the coveners "come together with your partner, loved one or friend and join your apple halves together with the other. Let each half become the balance of the other so that all are whole. Take a moment to give silent thanks for the balance in your life." The coveners pair up and press their apple halves together to make a whole. They take a moment to give silent thanks.

The High Priestess says "as the apple seeds form the pentagram, the symbol of our faith and the seed of life that has brought us to this point of balance, let us now eat of the fruit given for us". Everyone can sit round now and eat their apples and talk through amongst themselves what they see as having balance in their lives. The apple cores can be put into the cauldron and buried after the circle has been dismantled.

Consecrate and then have the cakes and ale then close the circle. Follow up with a feast.

26ᵗʰ March

10 ways to determine the right coven for me

With Paganism growing as quickly as it is, it's no wonder that there are so many enquiries from seekers and people interested or curious about Paganism in general. But as a person new to the Wiccan and Craft community, how do you determine what coven or group is right for you?

Making a commitment to learning about Wicca can, and should, be a life changing decision and so you want to make sure the group you choose to work with meets your needs and that you meet theirs. Working with a group is a two way street and you get back as much as you give of course. Anyone who's worked with a Wiccan, Witchcraft or magickal group of almost any description will tell you that when done properly, the relationships you develop are deep seated, powerful, emotional, psychic and lifelong. You all become spiritual partners, soul families, and it's a very special, caring and supportive relationship. So your choices in connecting with a potential group of people that 'gel' with you cement that special relationship even further. So what can you look for to determine which group is right for you before you commit?

First things first. You.
1. What are your needs and expectations?

Exactly what interests you? Is it Wicca or Craft? Is it ceremonial magick, spell-work, divination or something else from the myriad of esoteric practices? To be even more precise, does it feel right to you to be absorbed in an eclectic form of the Wiccan religion or a very precise and designated tradition such as Gardnerian? Instead would you prefer to work toward a more shamanic practice, perhaps one that focuses on the Kabala or eastern spirituality? Take some time to describe, in writing, exactly what you feel comfortable learning about as this will prove invaluable as a measure of 'fit' with prospective groups.

2. What are your values?

What are three life values you hold dear and live your life by? In other words, what are the three main principles, laws, or value sets that you want to live your life to?

3. What is the most important thing you want to gain from joining a group or coven?

This might sound like a daft question because you might think the answer's obvious, but is it? Think about what you want from a group. Is it companionship, teaching, guidance, answers to questions, to teach, social support, psychic support? What is the single most important reason why you want to join a group?

4. How much are you prepared to commit to the group in terms of time, effort and loyalty?

It's all too easy to jump into a new venture without thinking through what the commitment involves. Review seriously and realistically your availability in terms of time. What nights/days do you have free that you can devote to the group and its activities? What's your track record with joining new ventures? Do you get enthusiastic and then slowly get bored and neglect it? Do you commit to a group and stick with it no matter what? Think through exactly what your long term commitment to a group can be.

Now the group
5. What do they describe themselves as?

What does the group call themselves? Wiccan? Eclectic? Shamanic? Alexandrian? Egyptian focused? Indigenous etc? The way a group labels itself should give you a clearer view of how they practice and what style of function they have. You can now test this against your answers to question 1.

6. What are the underpinning values and ethos that frame how they operate?

This is really important because if the group can't articulate what their underpinning ethos or value set is then how can you decide if they what they stand for, their behaviours and their approach to life, fits with yours? Ask them to explain what they see as being important behaviour. How do they deal with conflict within the group? How do the value each other and then test this against your personal value set from question 2.

7. How does the coven or group teach?

Do they teach students through the traditional face to face method or do they deliver teaching online or via correspondence? Do they have a one to one mentoring provision or do they follow the apprenticeship model? Each of these ways of teaching has its strengths and weaknesses and the key is to choose a group which teaches the way that meets your needs. Do you need the personal and social support that comes with face to face teaching? Do you need the freedom to study that an online or correspondence program offers? Would you feel more comfortable with an apprenticeship style of learning?

8. How do they practice?

Simple but valuable question this one. One of the most important questions many people have but are afraid to ask is if the group practices skyclad (nude). Working nude for many people is very confronting and you need to get these issues out in the open before you commit. What other forms of practice do they have that either fit or clash with your values? Do they conduct the Great Rite actually or symbolically? Do they do all their rituals in a remote location and you have no transport? Do they expect payment for lessons and if so how much and why?

9. Do they have a hierarchy of authority related to degree structure or are they more democratically structured?

Some groups use a traditional three degree structure and this has an impact on your ability to be initiated through different levels. Others have a more open and democratic system where leadership is shared. This may have an impact and a requirement on you to write and lead rituals at some point and if so, can you do this? For those groups with a degree structure (some of which may have several degree levels like Golden Dawn for example), what are their policies and protocols around achieving those levels and what are the expectations about how you behave toward members of different levels?

10. Do the people and the group 'feel' right?

This is the most important question of all and one that requires you to use your gut instinct over your rational thought processes. Even if the group sounds perfect, their procedures and practices appear above board and sound and their reputation is outstanding, if your gut instinct tells you something's not right, then something's not right. It may be that this 'something' is not necessarily bad but just may be that the group is not the one for you. It may be that you've picked up on some underlying vibrations and energy that resists your own. Whatever the reason, if your instinct tells you to walk away, then walk away. There will be another group somewhere that's your home, just waiting for you to arrive.

2nd April

Are Wiccans the party faithful on polytheism?

Read any material on Wicca and it will tell you that Wicca is a polytheistic religion and its practitioners honour many different Gods and Goddesses. That's the party line but do we all tow it? Let's explore what polytheism actually is briefly and then we'll look at whether we really do it or not.

Polytheism's manifesto says that Wiccans honour many different deities, often across many different pantheons. Thus dependent on the circumstances, or indeed just how you may feel on that particular day, you might choose to honour or invoke a Roman God. But on another day you might work with a Greek Goddess, or maybe a Celtic God, or a Norse Goddess. The point is that you have the ability to choose from a broad range of deities depending on what divine attributes you need or that suits the event. A veritable smorgasbord of options, or to use our political analogy, you're faced with a broad range of presidential nominees from whom you can pick and choose dependent upon your political desires on any given day.

None of those Gods or Goddesses are the *President* by the way because if there was a single *President God or Goddess*, we'd be back to monotheism and the honouring of a single, all important deity. Obviously that's not what Wicca is a about. We do not honour a single God or Goddess and if we did so, we'd place ourselves in the same *theistic* boat as monotheistic Christians in terms of having a single divine presence. So that's not our campaign manifesto, or is it?

I'm going to upset the campaign trail here and suggest that far too many of us tend to favour the *Presidential* version, or at least one similar to it. Many Wiccans support the notion of the divine President and the First Lady concept or to be more precise, the President and Consort. We talk about the "Lord and Lady" in our rituals frequently and we often develop a relationship with a patron and matron God and Goddess and these two deities become our favourites. Nothing wrong with that at all... until we get so used to the routine "Lord and Lady" and get so focused on our patron and matron deities that we forget that it's not a pair of divine beings we're supposed to be honouring but a whole range of them. That's duotheism, not polytheism.

Now, just to confuse matters slightly, there's also pantheism, (and in fact quite a range of 'theisms') and I challenge you to go and learn a little about that definition in the light of this entire concept to broaden your understanding of this whole campaign debate. But I digress, (the smoke screen candidates use to divert people from the real issue!)

I'm not saying that we shouldn't use the term "Lord and Lady" or that we shouldn't have patron and matron deities. Far from it. What I am saying, is that in terms of "Lord and Lady", we need to always remember that this is a phrase that's supposed to represent not just a male and female divine pair but the broadest range of Gods and Goddesses. It's a term that asks us to consider that we are honouring all Gods and Goddess, both female and male and that "Lord and Lady" is just an easier way of addressing and talking to the entire realm of Wiccan deities.

With reference to patron and matron deities, while it's wonderful to have favourites, we must never forget that there are a whole range of candidates out there who deserve our attention and who have some fantastic manifestos of their own that can support our spiritual agenda.

So in conclusion, let's not forget as we walk this campaign trail of a spiritual life, that the Wiccan manifesto clearly states we're polytheistic, not duotheist or heaven forbid monotheistic. Let's not forget that we honour, we invoke and we work with a huge variety of divine candidates and that our ongoing votes should be deposited in the ballet box of the God or Goddess with whom we need to work that day and that tomorrow we can vote for another, equally as valid and important deity.

9th April

'Being' Wiccan instead of 'doing' Wicca

In learning about and practicing Wicca, do we focus so much on 'doing' Wicca that we forget about also 'being' Wiccan and knowing why we're doing what we do? I've been looking at Druidry and a thought struck me about one of the differences between Druidry and Wicca. At the risk of upsetting someone's apple cart, I'm going to suggest that as Wiccans, we often focus quite heavily on 'doing' Wicca but sometimes forget to just 'be' Wiccan. Let me explore that point for you.

In Wicca, we often focus very heavily on our practice and indeed when learning Wicca, a fundamental of that training is to 'do' Wicca as well as to 'know about' Wicca. This is fine and I certainly agree that in order to be trained appropriately, there absolutely has to be a balance between the 'doing' and the 'knowing about', or theory. You can't fully understand ritual for instance unless you participate in ritual. It's a bit like learning how to drive. It's not all theory and so you can't drive a car just by reading how to drive a car, you actually have to drive the car.

But do we get so wrapped in 'doing' Wicca, conducting rituals, celebrating the festivals through the wheel of the year, doing esbats and so on that we begin to see Wicca as just a set of practices rather than a religion? Do we get so hooked up on 'doing' it all that we forget about simply 'being' Wiccan?

If Wicca is a religion, then by its very definition, it should also be a way of life, a philosophy for the way we conduct ourselves every day and night of the year. In other words, a way of 'being'. A religion is of course a system for honouring its deity(s) and that is the practice or the 'doing', but religion is also a definition of who you are through its philosophical approach to life. "I am Wiccan" shouldn't just mean I conduct a few rituals and think that's OK. That's not 'being' Wiccan. If I were 'being' Wiccan, every day of my life would be in service to, in honour of and reverence to, my Gods and Goddesses. With our hands on our hearts, can we say that we live our lives that way every day?

Druidry by comparison doesn't always define itself as a religion. Instead it defines itself simply as a philosophy and as a way of living. One can be a Druid and have fairly fluid views on what constitutes deity and while it's fair to say that Druidic tenets engage with deity, the definition of deity is much more up to the individual. Thus it's far more loose than Wicca and isn't defined by a set of practices locked to festivals dates. One can follow Druidry without slavishly adhering to patterns of ritual. So one can 'be' a Druid simply by living life with an everyday behaviour set that reflects the Druidic philosophy. Druidry is thus more relative to the 'why' of life rather than the 'how'.

Having noticed this difference, I really did begin to question if we sometimes practice Wicca because that's the way we were taught or because that's what the books or religion supposedly demands of us rather than live our lives 'being' Wiccan. Wicca has to be more than just a religion. It has to be the philosophy that shapes my life and behaviour every day, in every way. I don't want to just 'do' Wicca, I need to 'be' Wiccan. Wicca isn't just a bunch of sabbats and esbats and a defined system of honouring the divine. It should also be my guideline for who I choose to be, every day, all the time. So I leave you with two questions. Do you really understand why you do the Wiccan things you do? And secondly, are you 'doing' Wicca or 'being' Wiccan?

16th April

Circle etiquette; what to do and not do in the circle

If you look on the internet, you'll find a whole host of 'recipes' on how to cast a circle and the rituals you can do. But there's much less information on the etiquette and manners that are expected when you are inside the circle.

Now if you're working as a solitary, you could argue that it doesn't matter about manners because you're the only one in the circle. Well, let's blow that idea out of the water straight away. You're not the only one in the circle at all. The quarter elementals are there with you and even more importantly, so is the Lord and Lady. Why else are you holding the circle? Would you be on your best behaviour if someone important came to share your home with you? Probably. Well that's exactly what the Gods and Goddesses are doing. They're sharing your circle with you and in fact the main reason you should have cast it in the first place was to honour them, and that means being on your best behaviour and minding your circle manners.

Manners are equally important when you visit someone else's coven and work with them in their circle. The old adage 'when in Rome...' works really well here with the exception that if they expect you to do something you don't feel comfortable with, respectfully decline. If you break all the rules of circle etiquette and are rude or dismissive, you simply won't be invited back so better to be safe than sorry. So what are some of the manners and etiquette expectations you should be aware of?

There's two sets of rules really. The more traditional rules come from original circle expectations demanded by early Wiccans. The contemporary rules are those expected by more eclectic Witches as they conduct probably more flexible rituals.

The More Traditional Must Do's
- Wear robes of a certain colour dependent on your degree level,
- Go skyclad (naked) where the rites require it,
- Wear a single piece of jewellery significant with your degree level/rank,
- Walk only in a deosil (sunwise) direction around the circle,
- Always address people in the circle by their Craft or magickal name even if you usually use their 'everyday' name at other times.

The More Traditional Must Not's
- Do not wear a watch or any other jewellery in circle,
- Never turn your back to the altar,
- Do not leave the circle until it is dismantled,
- Do not walk in a widdershins (anti-sunwise) direction unless you are dismantling the circle,
- Never enter a circle if you have not been initiated or without first answering the challenge.

The More Contemporary Must Do's
- Wear whatever you would like in circle but most participants wear a simple robe used only for circle work,
- Show respect for the fact that you are in a sacred space,
- Respect and follow the ritual actions of the host coven, (when in Rome etc),
- Whenever the ritual leader says "blessed be" as part of a ritual, you repeat the same term,
- Whenever the ritual leader says "so Mote it be" as part of a ritual, you repeat the same term,
- If you do not wish to sip from the wine chalice, kiss the front of it instead,
- It is quite acceptable to laugh when in the circle (except during meditations).

The More Contemporary Must Not's
- Never take a mobile phone into the circle,
- Do not enter the circle under the influence of illicit drugs or alcohol,
- Do not leave the circle until it has been dismantled unless absolutely necessary
- Never bring guests with you to a circle without permission from the ritual leader,
- Do not enter the circle when you are angry or upset. (The negative energy can be quite destructive to others present),
- No smoking in the circle,
- No eating or drinking in the circle except for cakes and ale or magickal workings,
- Do not perform individual magickal workings for your own needs inside the circle unless you have first discussed this with your fellow coveners,
- Never feel pressured to participate in any activity that makes you feel uncomfortable or unsafe.

OK, so with that list of do's and don'ts, you now have a much clearer idea of how you should behave when in circle. The simple thought to bear in mind when in your own circle or that of another coven is respect. If you always remember that the circle is a sacred space where the act of ritual participation demands your respect, where the Gods and Goddesses expect your respect and where the hosts would appreciate your respect, then you can't go far wrong.

23rd April

Cut the history lessons; just teach me the Wiccan juicy stuff!

Now and again students ask why they're expected to learn about Wicca's history (all the 'boring stuff') before they get into the 'juicy stuff' like magick, circle casting and working with the elements. Good question! Why don't I just jump straight in and teach some 'juicy stuff', after all that's what Wicca is isn't it?

I've learnt over the years to curb my own frustration when I get this question and I usually come back with something like "if you were learning how to drive a car, would you expect a good instructor to give you the keys, let you get in the car and drive straight down the first available freeway? Or would you expect them to sit with you in the car, explain the pedals, the seatbelt, the road rules, spend time getting you used to the feel of the clutch, help you manipulate the steering, the indicators, the pedals and watch the traffic and pedestrians all around you simultaneously, *before* they let you lose on the freeway?"

When anyone is teaching a skill set or knowledge set, particularly one as strong as a religion, a magickal system, a new life choice or a self improvement program (and isn't Wicca all of those things?) they have a responsibility to ensure that they teach not just the 'how' but also the 'why'. Wicca isn't just a bunch of actions that you do, it's also a life choice you make and a way to feel about life. You don't just 'do' that, you 'are' that. So it makes sense that a good teacher will spend the time to lay the appropriate foundations first so that the student's 'doing' is based on a sound understand of why they're 'doing'.

With that sound understanding, the student is also more able to modify the 'doing' into something that makes more sense to them. As an example, if I asked you to modify your lawn mower so that it didn't just cut grass but now also cut hedges, you probably wouldn't be able to modify it without having an understanding about how lawn mowers worked. So getting clear teaching on foundations helps the student modify and make more informed personal choices later on.

One other point that's worth noting is that teachers feel much more inclined to teach when the student genuinely wants to learn. Bear with me here because this is important. Most teachers do what they do because they love their task and teaching Wicca is no different. It is one of the joys of my life to offer information and skill development to people willing to give it a go. On top of that, Wicca is a religion whereby teachers generally provide that teaching free of charge (or they might ask for enough just to cover expenses but that's about it) and Oak and Mistletoe is no exception here. All our teaching is free and the costs are born by me because that's what I ethically believe is important and it's my contribution to the religion and to the students. But, and here comes the clincher, learning something as powerful as a religion, as a magickal system, as a life choice and a self improvement program takes dedication, tenacity and dogged determination. Achieving all that doesn't come in 2 weeks, or 3 months or even in 8 months. It comes after years of practice, years of dedication, years of trial and error and loyalty and a love of deity and nature. For a teacher to give that level and length of service to a student, free of charge and with absolute devotion, they need to know the student is serious. So getting the 'boring stuff', all the foundations and the 'why' sorted first helps the 'how' fall into place much more easily for the student over all those years. Like the driving instructor, a good Wiccan teacher probably wouldn't let you loose on the spiritual freeway before giving you some basic instruction first. Wiccan teachers have a responsibility to look after your religious safety and well being before they encourage you to take a spiritual joyride.

30th April

Samhain/All Hallows

A Greater Sabbat and an Earth Cross-Quarter Day
Northern Hemisphere October 31st
Southern Hemisphere April 30th
Seasonal Relevancy
Summer's already losing its power and people are preparing for the long winter ahead by making preserves from the harvest like jams and pickles and chutneys. They're also slaughtering all but the animals which will be used for breeding next season's stock because in the harsher earlier times, many of the weaker animals wouldn't have survived the chill of winter and there wasn't usually enough food to keep them all alive anyway. This is the time of the final harvest of the crops, the root and surface vegetables and the last of the fruit.

Mythological Relevancy
Samhain (pronounced Sow-ayne) is without doubt the most important sabbat of the Wiccan faith. While some covens might celebrate other festivals on the closest weekend to the date, this sabbat is usually always celebrated on the actual date even if coveners have to get up for work the next morning!

It's a sombre festival that celebrates the dead and marks the time when the veil between the world of the mundane and that of the Spirit is at its thinnest. This is the Wiccan New Year and at sunset, when neither the old nor new year exist and thus when time stands still, humans can commune with their ancestors and loved ones who've passed over.

Popular Traditions

While this sabbat celebrates our relationship with our ancestors and with the dead, it's not a frightening or sad occasion. It is a time to feast on the last of the harvest foods and to make ready for the cold times ahead. Many Wiccans lay an extra place or two at the feast table so that their departed ancestors and spirits can share in the festivities.

You can carve jack-o-lanterns from pumpkins to honour the Witches and other religious practitioners and followers who've been persecuted for their faith over the centuries. Pay any debts, settle your quarrels and prepare for a few weeks of quiet solitude and meditation.

A Contemporary Samhain Ritual

Decorate the circle perimeter with flowers and lay seasonal fruits and vegetables on a black cloth on the altar. These traditionally include apples, pomegranates, pumpkins, nuts and seeds. For the cakes and ale have apple cider and gingerbread. Ensure there's sufficient for those present as well as for absent friends and loved ones who may join us from the spirit world. Have a piece of paper and a pen available for each person present and have a knife available to slice an apple. Light a bonfire at the centre of the circle or have a cauldron with a candle inside it.

Cast the circle as normal if there are no visitors present, otherwise, omit the circle casting.

Have a discussion about Samhain and its meaning with those present. When that's concluded, begin the ritual by standing before the altar and saying "now is the time of change between the passing of the seasons. At this time of year the gates between the worlds are open. We call upon our ancestors and our loved ones, to pass through and join with us at this time. We invite them to delight in celebration with those they love."

Take an apple from the altar and slice it in half across the middle so that the star of the pips and core is evident. Place the two halves on the pentacle and hold it aloft over the altar saying "this is the fruit of life, which is also death".

Slice the apple into pieces, one for each person present plus one for visiting spirits. Go round the circle and offer a piece to each person. Ask them as they eat the apple to think of loved ones, including pets, who have passed on.

If using a candle in a cauldron instead of the central bonfire, light the candle using a lit taper from the spirit candle. Offer each person a piece of paper and a pen and ask them to think about an aspect of themselves they are uncomfortable with. This might be a bad habit, perhaps they get angry too quickly, upset too easily or spend money unwisely. It might be a behaviour or a thought pattern which does them a disservice and that they would like to eradicate. Ask them to write this on their paper and then fold it closed with a single fold.

In turn, each person offers their unwanted aspect to the flame. Ask them to consider that as the flame burns the paper away, they are offering this unwanted aspect to the Divine so that it can be changed and removed. This is a way of recognising issues of self detriment and deciding to let that issue leave and be replaced instead with something more productive.

Consecrate and then have the cakes and ale and then close the circle. Have a Samhain feast that includes the traditional foods from the altar. Ensure there's a fully set place at the feast table for any spirit visitors. When the feast is over, lay a spare plate of food (not leftovers) outside the front door overnight to bring sustenance to any passing spirits.

7th May

I'm a solitary; how do I get invited to a coven's festival?

Many Wiccans and Witches choose to work alone. They do so sometimes even after they've been initiated into a coven for a huge variety of reasons and that's quite legitimate. But, what if you work alone at home yet now and again want to attend the sabbat of a local coven? Can you do that and if so how?

Just like a party, a wedding or any other celebration of people you don't know, it would be pretty bad form if you gate crashed, even if you really loved weddings or birthday parties, or even if you did actually know someone there. The same is true of the sabbats held by covens. Many covens hold what's called 'open' festivals or sabbats where local Pagan friendly people are welcome to attend either through invitation or because they know someone in the coven already. Just a quick point of clarification here. The sabbats are the festivals that celebrate the eight Wiccan liturgical events throughout the year, a bit like Christmas and Easter for Christians. Esbats by comparison are the regular rituals, often held on a full or new moon, and they are usually only held for coven members.

If you want to strike up a relationship with a coven that holds open festivals but not actually become a member of the group, then you need to do your homework and be up front. Some covens simply won't allow this unless you're committed to their tradition or their way of doing things. Other covens will welcome you with open arms but will want to know a little about you first, maybe meet you before a festival to make sure you 'fit' with them and they with you. The final decision on attendance at a festival by an 'outsider' belongs to the coven leadership so you need to be on your best behaviour and make a good impression or they'll never invite you. Just like that wedding or party invite, you don't get one unless the wedding or party organiser thinks you'll fit in and should be there.

So how do you find a coven that might let you attend their festivals? This is where your homework comes in. Check out local web sites, Pagan supply shops and the local Pagan related organisations to see what covens are in your area. Witchvox is a really good start and you can find the site here at www.witchvox.com. The site is a great resource for locating covens and groups in your area no matter where you are in the world.

When you do this, make sure you know what style or tradition of Wicca you're akin to. It's no good approaching a fundamental Gardnerian coven if your preference is for an eclectic Egyptian sympathetic style. Similarly, if the group you approach is Asatru and you love a more traditional Alexandrian focus, then you're just not going to fit. Make sure you can explain what you want, what you feel is important and what style of Wicca appeals to you so that when asked (and you will be!) you can be clear, articulate and up front.

Your next step is simply to ask. Email, or telephone the coven contact if a number is provided, and politely ask if you would be able to attend any open festivals the coven might hold in the future. Explain that you prefer solitary work and why and talk through how you'd like some community feel to your practice on occasions. The coven leadership will probably ask to meet you first, probably over a cuppa in a public place somewhere before they offer you an invite. If you can offer a reference from a past Wiccan teacher or a local practicing Wiccan the coven leadership might know of, they may be a little more accommodating to your request especially if that reference is someone they respect. Be prepared for questions and to be 'on probation' for a few months. Wiccans are notorious for being a little hesitant to allow newbies into the fold and that's not necessarily because they think you're a nasty kind of person but because they've heard it all before from people who declare they want to be a part of something and who then never turn up!

Finally, when you do get an invitation, do two things. Accept or respectfully decline giving a reason why you can't attend and secondly, be polite when you get there. A coven leader takes a risk inviting a new person to a festival because they never really know how things will pan out so please respect their trust. If you can't attend, let them know in good time and explain why. Ask if you could attend the next festival instead.

Before you do attend, make sure you've asked beforehand if you need to bring anything with you. Most festival attendees will bring a plate of food to share and they might also be required to bring items for the ritual as well. If you're requested to contribute with something like this, please do. Coven leaders usually don't charge to teach and they cover allot of the ritual and coven costs themselves out of pure dedication so blatant freeloaders won't be appreciated for too long. Check also if robes are required or if the ritual will be done in street clothing.

Finally, when you get there, it's a case of 'when in Rome...' Show respect for the ritual, for those present and follow instructions. Unless the ritual involves something that makes you feel particularly uncomfortable or is simply immoral or illegal, it's good manners to 'follow the leader' and do what everyone else does. If all that goes according to plan, then hopefully they'll invite you back again and you'll have started a warm and friendly relationship of Wiccan community support.

14th May

How to dedicate yourself to the Wiccan deities

I'm often asked by solitary students if they can dedicate themselves because they can't go through a traditional initiation. The answer of course is yes if they feel the time is right. The real question is how.

Like initiation, dedication is not something to be taken lightly. It's not like choosing which breakfast cereal to have that morning! Dedicating yourself to the Divine is a serious commitment to your religion. Just as a nun or Islamic student dedicates themselves to their religious duty, so too do dedicants of Wicca. With a dedication, you are in effect promising that you will live your life according to Wiccan virtues. You promise to adhere to Wiccan laws, all the while committing to behaviours, values and practises that are sympathetic to the tenets of Wicca. You're entering the Wiccan family and pledging your faith and future to the Gods and Goddesses. Probably a little more serious a decision than "is it Weetbix or Cocoa Pops this morning?"

So having spent considerable time contemplating the significance and magnitude of the decision, once made the next action is to prepare and actually do it. The Seeker's Guide to Learning Wicca[1] which can be found either at Amazon or through the Oak and Mistletoe bookshop details a dedication rite in full so I won't repeat that here. Suffice to say however that there are some inclusions to a dedication right that enhance it and magnify its impact.

The first important thing is to make it personal to your own needs. So while you can use a published ritual such as that in the Seeker's Guide or even in one of Scott Cunningham's books, I'd encourage you to add or modify it with some words that mean something special to you and perhaps even some actions that make the rite your own. Perhaps you have a special tree in your back garden you'd like to do the ritual under, perhaps you grandmother taught you some Craft secrets and you want to wear the bracelet she gave you, perhaps you read some words by a poet which touched your heart so you use those.

The second thing is to choose your timing. Even though you may now have decided that you're ready, it can magnify the impact of the ritual significantly if you delay and work towards it. The anticipation, the planning, the preparing can all go a considerable way to elevating its purpose, to making it exciting and exhilarating. Good things come to those who wait my Mum used to say.

Choose a date that is significant to you. My own initiation was on a blue moon and for me that was very special. You might choose to do the ritual on your birthday, perhaps on Samhain, perhaps on the shortest day of the year, perhaps on a date with a significant number sequence like 09/09/09. Numerology is a fascinating divinatory process and esoteric practice in which different numbers have different vibrations. If you can use numerology to define your dedication rite, you may well be tuning into much more intense and meaningful energies that any other date might have missed.

If you want to begin the process of collecting your Wiccan tools and use those, now's the time to do that and your dedication might be the time to consecrate the tools as well. Doing both rites together can enable you to begin your Wiccan way of life with not just your commitment to the Gods and Goddesses but also a set of tools to help your practice thereafter.

If you have a friend or partner who is also Wiccan sympathetic, there's no reason why you can't combine your dedication ritual into a double ceremony. This gives you the opportunity to prepare together (or you can still both have separate rites but do them simultaneously) and the fellowship you share can significantly increase the value of your rituals later on. Sole rituals are wonderful but shared rituals are often much more powerful.

Finally, enjoy yourself! While your dedication is a serious commitment, it need not all be sombre. Make sure your ritual is fun and brings you joy. Inject it with some laughter, with some actions and words that make you happy and show you just how special you really are. Remember, this is a joyous occasion where you're entering a wonderful new phase of your life. Make some great memories with your very special dedication ritual.

[1] Treleven, Amethyst (2008). *The Seekers Guide to Learning Wicca: Training to First Degree for the Southern Hemisphere*, Oak and Mistletoe: South Australia.

[1] Treleven, Amethyst (2008). *The Seekers Guide to Learning Wicca: Training to First Degree for the Northern Hemisphere*, Oak and Mistletoe. South Australia.

21st May

If finding Wicca is like going home, where's the floor plan?

So many times we hear people say that for them finding Wicca was like going home. But I'm curious. If that's the case, where's the floor plan for this home? What does 'home' look like? In other words, what actually is 'home'?

I think this is important because what I think is home is not necessarily what someone else thinks is home and yet we all seem to be talking about going to the same home. Is it the same though? Let's take the analogy a step further to illustrate my point. I live in a house on the side of a hill that has four bedrooms, two living areas, gorgeous wooden floor boards, hideous cracks in the kitchen ceiling, a tiny and very useless laundry and has views across to the sea to die for. It's a huge house and I quite like it. One of my friends lives in an apartment on the fifth floor of a building in the centre of the city that's very modern, has views over city rooftops, is tiny, is concrete, is worth more than double my house but is a quarter the size. Yet another friend lives in a hundred year old house with a kitchen the size of my wardrobe but with the most amazing cathedral ceilings and an atmosphere about it that I utterly adore. We all like our own homes but each one of them is different. What's even more important is that none of us would trade with each other for anything!

So we're all 'home' but that home is really different for each of us. Surely Wicca as 'home' is just the same isn't it? What I see as being my Wiccan home is probably going to be slightly different than what you see as being your Wiccan home. Our life stories and experiences are different and this has led each one of us to a different space in our lives that helps direct what our Wiccan home floor plan should be like. While as Wiccans, we all tend to believe in the basic fundamentals of Wicca (that our floor plan will have walls, floors, windows, a roof, a bathroom, a kitchen etc), we each have preferences about the exact details of that floor plan (the size of the kitchen, cedar windows versus aluminium, two bathrooms instead of one, beige carpet in the lounge instead of exposed floorboards etc). So we all have the fundamentals of the floor plan like the Rede and a belief in deity but how we individually vary and express our Wiccan floor plan may be different. The question is, is this OK?

For me, the answer to that has to be yes. Inclusive Wicca clearly states that each person has the right to their own relationship with deity and that this is as it should be. I firmly believe that not only do we have that right, but that we also have the *responsibility* to manage that relationship. In other words, not only do we have our own Wiccan floor plan, but we're also the sole architects of that floor plan. We can inherit a floor plan given to us by our Wiccan teachers but we have the responsibility and ability to modify the floor plan to meet our own needs. I guess the art of that modification, of being your own architect, comes after learning about the fundamentals of Wicca and from learning about your own needs so that you're then best trained and qualified to begin drawing up your own Wiccan home floor plan.

So Inclusive Wicca says we're all Wiccan architects either qualified or still in school training to be architects. My two questions to you at this point are simple. What does your Wiccan home floor plan look like and are you ready to take responsibility to draw it up?

28th May

Choosing a Craft or magickal name

OK, so you've read the books and been told that most Witches and Wiccans will need to choose their Craft or their magickal name. 'Craft' and 'magickal' can mean the same thing depending on the group, tradition or system you're learning. So what's a Craft name and how do you choose one? Let's get to that in a second, but first we just need to decide if you actually have to have a Craft name or not.

Depending on the tradition you favour, your Craft name is either given to you by a coven member, by the deities, or you choose one yourself. Alternatively, some traditions determine that you have a 'public' name and a 'private' name known only by you and the Gods and Goddesses. Let's make it simple though. If you follow an eclectic path you can have a Craft name or not choose to have one. The choice is yours. There's no rule that says "thou shalt be known by a Craft name from this day henceforth!"

The value in a Craft name is that it gives you the opportunity, often at the same time that you dedicate yourself to the Divine, to rename yourself with a title that you feel gives a more personalised and deeper description of who you are rather than what your Mum and Dad named you all those years ago. In other words, you get to choose what you should be known as before the Lord and Lady. This is actually a really special opportunity to redefine who you are so it's not to be taken lightly!

So a Craft name is a new label that identifies you before the Gods and Goddesses but it's a label you get to choose for yourself rather than have it dropped on you by parents who were never really sure of the person you were going to develop in to. Having a Craft name also identifies you within the Wiccan and Craft community and let's people know that you are Wiccan sympathetic. It's a 'tag' if you like that says "I am Wiccan" that other Wiccans and Witches can then identify with.

The really big question though is how to choose a name. To be honest, on many occasions, the name chooses you. A bit like cats and how they will either adopt you or not want to talk to you! If the name is yours, it will come to you. This means that usually, that name won't come to you till you're ready and then it will either simply jump out at you or gradually keep jumping on your lap until you decide you like it, again like a cat!

A couple of words of warning here. It's probably bad form to give yourself the name of a 'high' God or Goddess, someone like Gaia or Herne. That's almost tantamount to calling yourself God or Goddess even though in fact you are! It's much better to name yourself the daughter (or son) of a higher Goddess like Rhiannon. I'd also steer clear of the fluffy names like 'Lady Moonbeam of the Silver Goddess Tresses' or 'Starlight Speckled Robin' or something equally as ridiculous if I were you. You'll only get laughed at which may not be good for your self confidence!

You might want to represent yourself not with the name of a deity but with the name of something else that you have a strong association with. Perhaps a type of tree, a plant, an animal, a crystal, a time of year or a special place. There are so many options available to you and you don't have to stick with the earthly bound names like 'Jane', 'Robert' or 'Susan'. You can name yourself, and therefore be, anything you feel is right before the Lord or Lady.

So with all that, the choice to take on a Craft name or not is yours, as is the name you finally allow into your life and adopt as your own. You may also want to change it again when you go from first to second degree or you may want to stick with it for life. It's your choice, your name and you can do whatever you like. This is your opportunity to describe who you are with your name, probably for the first time in your life.

4th June

Do you really need Wiccan ritual tools?

It's true to say that most Wiccans and Witches would use ritual tools and in particular the athame, perhaps a wand and their book of shadows quite consistently and while some of this might be because they were taught this way, tools are by no means necessary. They do a wonderful job to enhance your Wiccan practice but of themselves, they aren't actually your practice, they just make it better. The danger with tools is that they can become the reason you practice rather than a help to your practice. When you can no longer cast a circle without your athame then something's wrong.

You are the conduit and generator of power, not the tools so if you begin to see them as necessary and that without them you can't operate, then you need to go back to the basics and start again. The best way to begin learning about Wicca and Witchcraft in the first place is to practice circle casting and so on using only yourself and nothing else. Cast the circle with your hand instead of an athame for example. If you can feel the power work through you, then your tools will just strengthen that.

Visualisation and meditation are cornerstone practices of Wicca and can be done without the need for any tools whatsoever. This is one reason why many teachers focus on these aspects early on in many Wiccan training programs. Master your inner talents and strengths and Wicca and Witchcraft will be enhanced then by your tools. Never let them become your practice; they merely focus and stretch your skills further.

11ᵗʰ June

Learning about Wicca without being in a coven

So you want to learn about Wicca and you can't, or prefer not to, join a coven to do so. Can you learn to 'be' Wiccan without training under a teacher? This is a really good question and you'll get a variety of answers depending on who you talk to.

Some teachers will say that you can't learn to be Wiccan unless you train under a good teacher. I'd suggest part of that statement is true. If you want to learn the fundamentals and practices of a particular group (or even tradition) then yes, you probably do need to learn under a good teacher of that group/tradition. But often, what teachers forget is that many people can be Wiccan without belonging to a particular tradition or group. For those people, they can learn on their own up to a certain level. We'll talk about that in a moment but first, let's consider something else.

The first thing to remember when you first start out is that you can learn 'about' Wicca from books, the internet and so on, but you can't learn to 'be' Wiccan unless you 'do' Wicca. The religion of Wicca isn't just a cognitive, knowledge thing, it's a practice, it's a way of life, it's a 'doing' thing. To be Wiccan, you don't just *know about* Wicca, you also *do* Wicca.

So that means if you want to learn about Wicca, then by all means read as many books as you can, visit as many web sites, watch the rituals offered at open festivals, talk/email and contribute to as many online forums as you can. But, if you want to learn how to *be* Wiccan, then you need to do all that *and* actually do it yourself. Have a go at rituals, have a try at writing a ritual, follow the scripts for circle casting offered in good books, listen and watch nature and work with it. *Do* Wicca, don't just read about Wicca.

Remember I said earlier that you can learn to a certain level on your own? Well that's certainly true and for many people that's perfectly good enough. But if you want to take your training to a whole new level, then you probably do need to train under a teacher and maybe work with a group. Honouring Wicca as a group lends a whole new layer of learning to everyone involved and not just because a community shares its knowledge with you. Working with a good group can give you the opportunity to see the real power of group magic, shared ritual and the magnificence of communal celebration. Working with a group of likeminded people makes the learning multiply exponentially for everyone and it's a wonderful thing!

However, take heart. If you can't or simply don't want to train with a teacher, you most definitely can learn, both about and to be, Wiccan. Just choose your sources of information carefully and above all *do it*, don't just read about doing it!

18ᵗʰ June

Winter Solstice/Midwinter/Yule

A Lesser Sabbat and a Sun Quarter Day
Northern Hemisphere December 21/22nd
Southern Hemisphere June 21/22nd
Seasonal Relevancy
　　This is the longest night of the year and the shortest day and winter's at its peak. It's cold and dark and animals are hibernating, the birds are silent and the plants are all dormant.

Mythological Relevancy
　　This festival marks the return of the sun with the cyclic story of the death of the Holly King (the king of the waning year) and the re-birth of his son the Oak King (the king of the waxing year).

Popular Traditions
　　Yule is a time to look forward to the return of the sun and the light and warmth that it brings. Although it's still cold, this time of year brings hope for a brighter future as we quietly celebrate the forthcoming warmth and prepare for the growth season.
　　Find a good size Oak log and decorate it with Ivy, (traditionally also with Holly and Mistletoe; Holly because it's an

evergreen and symbolises ongoing life while the seeds of Mistletoe, prevalent at this time of year, symbolise the sacred seed of new life). Light the log with an unburnt piece of last year's Yule log to symbolise the kindling light of the re-born sun. Save a small piece of this year's log from burning to use to light next year's log and spread the ashes of the burnt log on the garden.

A Contemporary Winter Solstice - Yule Ritual

Decorate the altar and the circle perimeter with Holly and Ivy leaves, golden garlands and lots of candles. There should also be a crown made from Oak leaves (these should be gathered in the previous summer, pressed and lacquered ready for Yule). Light a balefire in the centre of the circle and beside it, lay this year's new Oak Yule log and the piece from last year with which to light this year's log.

Cast the circle as normal if there are no visitors present, otherwise, omit the circle casting. The Oak King lays down in a foetal position in the Eastern quarter of the circle. The ritual leader then opens the rite by saying "this festival marks both the rebirth of the sun at the midpoint of winter and the rebirth of the Oak King as he returns to us each year. The Goddess, in all her glory, gives birth to the light of the sun above us and her son the Oak King before us. (Pointing to the baby Oak King laying on the floor in the east of the circle). The Holly King must die to make way for his son and the return of the light. We celebrate this night with the joyous birth of the Oak King!"

The coven maiden takes the Oak leaf crown from the altar and kneels before the baby Oak King saying "we honour thee, our newborn God". The Oak King rises to face her and she places the crown on his head. He stands before those gathered and says "I am reborn once more, and with me comes the light of the sun. I honour my father, the Holly King, the King of the waning year."

The High Priestess says; "All hail the Sun God!" Everyone says; "All hail the Sun God".

The ritual leader picks up last year's Yule log and hands it to the Oak King saying "as we honour the reborn sun God, let us also remember that life is a cycle of death and life. Here are the remnants from last year that we saved to honour this year. Oak King, Lord of the waxing year, rekindle the light of the sun".

The Oak King uses last year's log to light the new Oak log in the balefire. When the new Yule log is burning, he says "all hail the sun God!" Everyone says "all hail the Sun God".

Consecrate and then have the cakes and ale and then close the circle. Follow up with a feast and games beside the Yule balefire.

25th June

Do I have to do Wiccan rituals naked?

Ritual work done nude, or skyclad as its known (clad only in the sky), is often something that many prospective Wiccan students fear and they'll often ask "do I have to be naked in ritual?" Their question and fear is common and it deserves some clear answers. Working naked is something that many solitary Wiccans and covens choose to do, largely because Gerald Gardner suggested that the best way to stand before the Gods and Goddesses was in your natural state without the social trappings and potential hierarchies of clothing. Different clothes say different things about people and we often make assumptions about people based on what they're wearing which could be wildly wrong.

Look, there's a simple answer to this question and it's this. You NEVER have to do anything that makes you feel uncomfortable. Most traditional Gardnerian and Alexandrian covens ask you to go skyclad for the initiation ritual but many eclectic covens don't. Talk to your prospective coven about their robes or skyclad policy and make a choice that suites you. After all this is YOUR religion too!

2nd July

Questions to ask a prospective Wiccan teacher

So you've decided to go and find a teacher, good on ya! Now comes the hard part, actually finding an ethical teacher who's got enough experience in *doing* Wicca and not just knowledge *about* Wicca, who can actually teach properly and who's willing to teach you!

In another edition, I'll talk about how you can find a teacher but this time, let's focus on some questions to consider when you do locate a potential teacher. The first thing to realise is that just because you think they're the right teacher for you, they may not think you're the right student for them. Learning Wicca from a teacher is a two way street and it involves having a mutual relationship of respect and trust. Sometimes we just don't 'click' with people and although your potential teacher may sound perfect for you, they may not feel the same way about you. The trick here is simply to accept it and find another teacher instead.

But what questions do you ask of a possible teacher? How do you know if they're right for you? How do you make a judgement about their ethics, experience and teaching ability?

First up, good teachers are in demand so while there are good teachers who don't have lots of students, there are even more good teachers who have a sound, stable and loyal group of students. Find out how many students the teacher has and how long those students have been with them. Ask them lots of questions about their students and their teaching like;

- What's the maximum number of students you teach at any given time?
- How do you teach those students?
- How long is your teaching program?
- What is the teaching curriculum for your students?
- Does your teaching cost anything and if so why and how much exactly?
- How often are lessons?
- Where are your lessons held?
- What happens if a student has to miss a lesson?
- What's your protocol if a student is disruptive or simply doesn't fit in?
- How do you make sure that each student is learning as much as they need to?
- How did they learn about Wicca and when?

Obviously you'd want to know lots about the group as well before you commit to each other because the group approach is fundamental to a good fit between you and them. Think about your own needs first. Do you want to learn from the traditional viewpoint of a Gardnerian or Alexandrian group or would you prefer the flexibility of a more eclectic approach? Have you examined your own beliefs so that you can talk them through with the potential teacher to see if your ideas gel with theirs? Does your history of religious upbringing leave you feeling a little damaged and does a potential teacher need to know this? Do you have a measured and deliberate stand on whether you do rituals nude or clothed? Do you have any allergies or illnesses which might impact on your learning and later ritual work such as aversions to incense or perhaps even a choice not to drink alcohol which might mean you need to ask about how you'd participate in the Cakes and Ale ritual? It's really important that you think through your needs so that these are met when you finally find a good teacher.

More questions for your teacher too around simple things such as;

- What are their expectations on initiation or dedication?
- Can you participate in esbats before you commit to Wicca?
- Does the group have an affiliation with a broader body of Wiccans and if so who and what are their credentials?
- What contribution does your teacher and group provide to their local Wiccan community?
- Why did they choose to teach Wicca and what experience/expertise do they have to do so?
- Does the group have a Code of Ethics or a set of bylaws, a charter or anything similar?
- How does the group share responsibilities like contributing candles, ceremonial wine, taking care of any group funds and so on?
- Do you get to write rituals or only participate in rituals?
- Is casting the circle and leading rituals shared throughout the group or are these always conducted by the group leader or High Priestess?
- What happens if you want to leave the group?
- Does the group share rituals with any other group and how is this managed?

So many questions, so little time! However, it is important to really prepare and be honest with yourself and your potential teacher before you commit to a teaching program. If it all goes according to plan, you'll be developing a deep and loyal relationship with the teacher and the group and it's important to start this off on the right foot.

9th July

Setting up an altar at home

So you'd like to set up an altar at home somewhere, but where do you put it and what do you put on it? Many Wiccans have an 'official' altar that they use in their circle work and also an 'unofficial', everyday one they keep in use at home all the time. But before we get caught up on the details, let's just explore what we mean by the term 'altar'.

It's important to remember that when we talk about altars, we're not referring to the sort of heavy, ornately carved wood or stone structures you might see in churches. You know the ones I mean. The big tables that sit at the 'business' end of church, often draped with beautifully worked and complex tapestries or embroidered linens, weighed down by brass, silver or gold candelabras, bowls and other donated antiquities and artefacts. No no, nothing quite so grand.

While a circle altar might in fact be quite formal and reflect the requirements of both the Wiccan tradition in which it's being used and the festival or event that is occurring, home altars are often much less formal, much more relaxed and friendly. Your home altar is really a place where you can place your Wiccan ornaments and any pieces that represent the Gods and Goddesses. You might also have a candle or two there to honour the fire element, perhaps a shell you found when on the beach to represent water, some nice incense or a feather for air and maybe a bowl of salt for the earth element. Your altar can sit on an East or North facing wall depending on your preference, in fact it can be anywhere that feels right for you.

There are some real gains in having a readymade altar, always available. With a personal, always ready altar you can go to regularly;

- you strengthen your relationship with the divine because you'll usually remember to take a few moments, more often to talk with her,
- You have a central place of honour where you can position your Wiccan objects,
- You have a focal point for any meditative practice,
- You have a readymade place to conduct any magickal workings and hold magickal tools or equipment,
- You'll more than likely have the benefit of warm, comforting residual energy that builds in the location of your altar the more you use it.

While a personal, permanent altar at home is a wonderful way to keep your Wiccan practice constant, please remember some safety principles. If you have sharp objects (like an athame for instance) or candles and incense burning on your altar, always remember that while the Gods and Goddesses will be attracted to your place of honour and respect, so will small children and your pets. *Never* leave candles and incense to burn when you're not there and always make sure your altar items are safe from children, animals and even non Wiccan prying eyes who may not understand or appreciate how much you value your tools.

16th July

The dangers of being eclectic

So you want to learn about Wicca and you think that eclectic practice fits you much better than the long standing traditions like Gardnerian and Alexandrian? Maybe you're thinking the flexibility of eclectic Wicca gives you more latitude to do your own thing rather than sticking with a fixed set of practices? Hmmm maybe, but it also comes with some responsibilities and challenges.

Following traditions like Gardnerian Wicca give you a very firm framework in which to sit your practice. There's much less room to move in terms of bringing different ritual practice into your repertoire and if you're living in the southern hemisphere this can be a real problem largely because Gardnerian practice usually dictates you celebrate certain festivals at certain times regardless of the fact that we may be experiencing the opposite of what ecologically that festival is all about. In addition, if you're learning Gardnerian or Alexandrian Wicca, then given it's an initiatory practice, you'll need to be learning under the guidance of an initiated Gardnerian who knows their stuff. But, if you're not into the more strict practices that support the longer standing Wiccan traditions and you want to follow a more eclectic path, then the world's your oyster and you can do what you want, right? Wrong.

Regardless of the tradition you chose to align yourself with, Wicca still has some underpinning fundamentals that govern your practice. These include things like;

- Polytheism
- Wiccan Rede
- The Law of Return
- An underpinning prescription to honour yourself, others and the world around us.

"So what" I hear you say, "I can do all that within eclectic practice can't I?" Yes you can but you also need to be careful that you don't include a load of other stuff as well which is not Wiccan and still call yourself Wiccan. Let me explain.

Jane Doe considers herself to be an eclectic Wiccan. She celebrates the eight sabbats according to a fairly basic liturgical calendar and she also honours the Gods and Goddesses in esbats. She accepts the Law of Return and she always considers the Wiccan Rede. A model eclectic Wiccan, yep. However, she also loves the underpinning principles of Ramadan and so fasts during the Ramadan period as a means of preparing herself to be a better person. She also refuses to allow any meat or products derived from animals in the circle and she casts her circle using indigenous practices because she feels this brings her closer to her local ecological environment. Hmmm... Is Jane still Wiccan or has she created a new religion called 'Jane Doeism'? You've got to ask this question.

In my opinion, Jane has deviated from Wiccan practice by adding additional elements to it that aren't required and that in fact don't compliment the Craft but contrast with it. Ramadan, while a wonderful opportunity for seeking forgiveness, repentance and moving on to a better way of life, is centred around a patriarchal religion and seeks a period of prayer with that God. He is not one of the Gods that Wiccans would honour. Furthermore, to introduce indigenous practice from countries other than where Wicca originated is to weld different cultures/religious principles together and to create a new hybrid culture and religious principle set.

Let me say right now that I have no problem with anyone adding to their Wiccan practice, especially when it allows the practitioner to connect more fully with the Lord and Lady and with the local environment. No problem with that, but the situation changes when those additions change the fundamental practice and turn it into something else that's no longer Wiccan. If the additions move that religious practice away from Wicca and into something else, then the simple fact is that it's no longer Wicca but is in fact 'Jane Doeism. Jane's responsibility at that point is to change her self-label from Wiccan to Jane Doeism. There's absolutely nothing wrong with developing a set of religious practices that suit your own needs and honour who you are but you have a clear responsibility NOT to label that as something it obviously isn't.

So in conclusion this week folks, please think about how far from the underpinning principles of Wicca you might be travelling when you add additional elements of practice. As long as they support your Wiccan practice, that's OK but when they detract from it, then you're creating a new, personalised religion that you may need to re-label.

23rd July

What's the difference between divination and Wicca?

Having taught Wicca for quite some time now, I'm still shocked by the number of people (even those who label themselves as long term Wiccans) who don't seem to understand the difference between the tools of divination and the tools of Wicca. This is a real problem because using tools of divination doesn't automatically make you a Wiccan, in fact being Wiccan doesn't automatically assume you'll use tools of divination either! These tool sets, while being supportive of one another, are mutually exclusive. Let's separate them out first and then let's look at why they don't have to go together in your Wiccan 'toolkit'.

Let's take divination tools first. These include all manner of objects that help you see the world and events and people's lives more clearly. They include things like;

- Runes
- Tarot cards
- Crystal balls

- Angel cards
- Scrying mirrors
- Pendulums
- Witches runes
- Crystals

Divination tools are those objects that help you clear and use your third eye or help you focus more selectively on events or people through another plane. They are the simple tools that enable you to see what you might not be able to otherwise see about yourself, about other people or the world in general. Wiccan tools on the other hand include things like;

- Athame
- Wand
- Chalice
- Censor
- Boline
- Bell

There's heaps more tools of course and depending on the tradition that interests you, there may be some you 'must have' and some that are simply not necessary but might be nice to have. These tools are not used for divination and in truth are the artefacts of the religion. They're the tools that enable you to focus more clearly on your connection with the Gods and Goddesses. They help you get into a state of connection with the Lord and Lady and while they're not absolutely necessary to being Wiccan, they can often help with your religious practice.

So given then that divination tools help you see into different planes and Wiccan tools help your religious practice, can't they be all put together in the same toolkit? Well yes they can but they don't have to be. Let's see why.

There are many types of Wiccans. There's the very traditional Gardnerians and Alexandrians, the more flexible eclectics, solitary Wiccans, coven based Wiccans, Wiccans who are vegetarian, Wiccans who eat meat, Wiccans who use Tarot cards, Wiccans who explore numerology, Wiccans who prefer herb lore than tarot and so on. Just because you're Wiccan doesn't mean you also have to use Tarot cards, crystal balls, pendulums and so on. Many Wiccans prefer to follow their religious pursuits without the need for Tarot, star signs, numerology or whatever. They're perfectly happy just being Wiccan without also having to be 'fortune tellers'.

By comparison, there's a bunch of people out there who do love to use (some of whom are scamming you and some of whom are genuinely very good at what they do) Tarot, scrying mirrors, star signs or whatever to help you get a better insight into who you are, what your future may hold, what it may hold for others, what connections you have with Sprit world and so on. But those folks are not necessarily Wiccan, neither do they have to be. Many follow no faith whatsoever. This doesn't make their gift any less effective, it just means they're using the practices of divination outside a religious framework.

The simple fact is that you do NOT have to have a cupboard full of mystical looking crystal balls, rows of Tarot decks and star sign charts to be Wiccan. It's not a necessity of the practice but it's an add on. It's like a vegetarian doesn't have to eat carrots to be a vegetarian. They probably do but they do so because they like carrots and not because they have in order to be vegetarian.

So if you thought all Wiccans had to be 'fortune telling', all seeing, mystical and prophetic geniuses then think again. Wicca is a religion, not a practice of fortune telling. It's about connecting with the Lord and Lady and honouring our beloved planet and those around us. If you're also gifted and able to use divination tools, then so much the better but it's not a prerequisite to being Wiccan.

30th July

Imbolg/Candlemas

A Greater Sabbat and an Earth Cross-Quarter Day
Northern Hemisphere February 2nd
Southern Hemisphere July 31st
Seasonal Relevancy
　　Spring is on its way at last and we can very clearly see that the days have become longer and the warmth and light of the sun is returning. Imbolg comes from the ancient word meaning 'ewe's milk' and reminds us that this is lambing season. In addition, the grass is beginning to grow again and the spring flowers are just beginning to burst forth from the ground.

Mythological Relevancy
　　Imbolg is the time of the quickening. The baby Oak King is growing and the Goddess is a maiden once more. This sabbat belongs to the fire Goddess Brigid, who presides over healing, the well springs and the hearth.

Popular Traditions
　　Because this time of year is synonymous with new life, new ideas and new beginnings it's particularly relevant for initiations and dedications. Even more, it is a purifying time of year when we should clear out the old things that have held us back and make

room for brighter and healthier behaviours and actions for the growing season ahead.

Make a Brigid's Cross from straw, hang it on your front door as a protective charm and burn the old one from last year. Conduct rituals with candles to invoke the fire Goddess Brigid, and to symbolise the light of the longer days.

A Contemporary Imbolg Ritual

The altar is prepared as usual. A cauldron with at least one stone in it for each person present sits in front of the altar. Each covener should previously have been asked to bring a food donation of one tin or packet of non perishable food item with them. Also have a space, box or bag in front of the altar for people to offer this food donation into. Cast the circle as normal if there are no visitors present, otherwise, omit the circle casting.

The ritual leader addresses those gathered "welcome to all those who have gathered here today to celebrate the festival of Imbolg. Traditionally this is a time of year when we should be spring cleaning our homes and repaying old debts in preparation for the coming light of spring. Making sure we have completed these tasks allows us to be more emotionally free and prepared to take on the new challenges of the growing season ahead and thus develop ourselves along with the new light of spring".

"In these modern days of isolation where we don't always know, let alone see, our neighbours, today we will be focusing on community and how you can contribute to the people around you as you prepare to bring in that light of spring."

"The stone soup fable is a simple story that shows how a group of people can work together to support each other and bring joy and a sense of belonging to one another. The story goes like this..."

Some one reads the following fable out to the group.

A weary traveller, in the depths of winter, came into a dark village. His feet were sore and his stomach was empty. He walked, door to door, with nothing but a single copper coin to his name, and asked the villagers if he could buy some of their food. At each door, a gaunt villager told him that they were starving, unable to spare even a morsel of their winter stores.

Finally, the young man sat down in the centre of the square, aware of the eyes peeking at him from shuttered windows. He reached down, brushed some snow from a small rock beneath his feet, and lifted it. With a start, he leapt to his feet, looked up to the shuttered windows, cleared his throat and made an announcement. "You silly, starving people! How can you hide behind your walls, desperate for food when you have perfectly good stones like this laying all around you? Does but one of the women here have a good kettle she can loan me? I promise enough stone soup to feed her whole family if she loans it to me for the day!"

The washerwoman had a kettle frozen behind her house, a large kettle last used for stew at Christmas time, too large to use for her family's meagre meals and too small for laundry. She volunteered it, and the young man dragged it, full of snow, from the outdoor hearth it had occupied for a month to the centre of the square. Villagers, bored in the dark winter, gathered around to help the man start a fire and melt the snow and ice in the pot. They were all convinced he was nuts, but helped him nonetheless. It was a sleepy village, and his obvious lunacy was worth a few cold feet to observe.

Once the snow had melted, he lifted the stone high for all of the villagers to see and plopped it into the pot. "Stewus blueus magic rock" he chanted, "give us soup within this crock!" He walked three times around the pot and took a spoon someone handed him and dipped it n. Ever the diligent cook, he tasted the water and its mild aftertaste of Christmas stew and shook his head. "It's bland," he told them, "if only I had a bit of salt."

The butcher told him he had salt sitting in his salting pot, the remnants of salting the midwinter's catch, which had run out the week before. It was brown and hardened into one lump, but he'd give it to the man for free.

The man took his offer gladly, and added the brown lump to the pot. He again took a sip. "The magic is working" he told his audience, and, indeed, there was a faint smell of food coming from the pot. He sipped the soup again, and made a face. "It's too sweet! If only I had the ends of some turnips, or some radishes to give it some bite!"

Two women looked about and then went into their houses, coming out with half-rotten vegetables. The man carefully cut the rotted parts away and added the vegetables, greens and all.

There was no mistaking that it smelled like food now. The man tasted the soup, and said "it's missing something" and handed the spoon to the brewman's wife, who nodded, then scurried into the closed tavern, returning with a small burlap bag of barley. As she dumped it in, the wife of the mayor objected. "You can't have barley in soup without parsnips!" she declared, and produced a bunch of limp, greying parsnips, which she handed to the man, who skinned them, chopped them and plopped them in.

Another woman objected as well, adding a fat, dry onion to the broth, and another, and still another, each adding the small secret ingredient that made the soups they made at home 'perfect'.

Within an hour, the smell of the soup filled the square, and the people came from every crevice and corner with a bowl. The mayor of the town hailed the wanderer as their saviour and put him up in his own house after he and the villagers had filled their bellies with delicious, if odd-tasting, stone soup.

At this point, the ritual leader begins a discussion by suggesting that listening to that story leads us to consider a whole bunch of things. What might that story be teaching us? Perhaps it teaches us about community contribution, a spirit of togetherness, compassion, and that each little bit helps. Sometimes we need one person to start the chain of events off and it's often easier to ignore someone in need than to provide help.

The ritual leader asks those gathered "who or what is community? Is it the people around where you live? Is the community your work mates? Is it your coven/group friends? Perhaps it's the Pagan community? Or is the community your social group?"

The ritual leader addresses those gathered saying "like the kettle of stone soup in the story, here you will find a cauldron loaded with different stones. Stones and rocks are bounty from our Earth and each stone brings with it different Earth memories and contributions from Gaia. Each stone here is therefore a gift from Gaia and these gifts are yours to use wisely and appropriately. Each stone here also represents a contribution that you can make to your community."

"Take a moment now to think about who your community is and what contribution you can make to it. It may be that your contribution is to mow your elderly neighbour's lawn, to wash your friend's/partner's/parents' car, to visit that friend in hospital, to make the time to bring morning tea in for your colleagues at work, to donate a rug to a charity."

"When you have decided who your community is and what you can contribute to it, take a stone. Then spend a few moments to send your thoughts of contribution into that gift from Gaia."

"Now that you have all sent your thoughts into your stones. What do you think we need to do now? We need to enact the thoughts we just created."

Someone else addresses those gathered "Gaia, Mother Goddess of our planet, let these stones before us be the catalyst that brings about our intention. We ask that you hear our thoughts and help us create the reality. Help us donate our energies, our actions, ourselves to those around us, who mean so much to us and who help make us who we are. Let these stones remind us of our pledge to our community and ensure that we live up to our pledge. So mote it be."

Yet someone else addresses those gathered "as we go home to our families, to our friends, our work and our lives, let each of these stones remind us that we pledged here today to make a contribution. We pledged to offer something of who we are to help someone else be who they are. So mote it be."

The ritual leader addresses those gathered again "Imbolg comes from the ancient word meaning 'ewe's milk' and reminds us that this is lambing season. Ewes provide us with warm woollen clothing and with food. To honour Imbolg's ancient link with food and to further honour our commitment to community as in the stone soup fable, we have elected to donate some of our food to the larder of those less fortunate than ourselves. In sharing our food with others, we honour the Gods and Goddesses and the community of which we are part."

"Please take a moment now to place your food offering before the altar. As you do so, take a moment to remember those who are not always able to provide food for their own families."

Consecrate and then have the cakes and ale then close the circle. Follow up with a feast during which everyone considers those less fortunate than themselves who may be unable to feast.

6th *August*

Negative and positive energy

It's often crossed my mind that what one person sees as a negative energy may be positive energy for someone else and vice versa. For Australians, a simple question we often ask and discuss is that if a circle is cast in the traditional sunwise (deosil) direction because that reflects and works with the natural direction the sun takes across the sky in the northern hemisphere, then here in the southern hemisphere, we should be casting the circle in the opposite direction. In the winter sky, the sun clearly travels in a widdershins direction down under. So following traditional constructs, to cast a circle in a deosil direction would mean we would be dismantling energies, working against them rather than working with them. I offer this as a simple illustration that what one person sees as being a form of negative, or positive energy is not necessarily what is universally the case. So what I consider positive and constructive, you may consider negative and destructive yet we're both right in our own contexts.

However in exploring the mixture of energies more specifically, an eclectic practitioner must first determine in their own minds what exactly they are trying to achieve and what constructs of deity they deem are important. Their circle casting and other rites can then emphasise, reflect and revere their chosen deity construct.

With a clear picture in their mind of their belief, they can then develop a circle rite that reinforces their personal approach to deity. However, the real responsibility comes when the effects of those rites enter into their own lives, those of others and even more so when and if they begin teaching others the fundamentals of ritual development. First and foremost a ritual is effective when it reinforces your own beliefs even if those beliefs are in opposition to others. For instance Satanic, Christian or Muslim rituals may be in direct opposition to what someone considers appropriate but for the practitioners of those beliefs, those rituals are not just appropriate but also sacred.

Having said all that, a 'generic' Wiccan circle, cast by an eclectic practitioner needs to incorporate a number of elements that allow it to remain true to the faith it's supposed to be aligned with whilst not contradicting its own activity. For example, a Wiccan who sees themselves as a traditional Alexandrian would probably not be comfortable taking on aspects of Faerie construction or fundamentalist Dianic workings. This is where we concern ourselves even more with the concept of mixing energies. To bring in one form of energy for a specific reason, or indeed because you know no different or have been taught a specific way, can be counterproductive when you call in an opposing set of energies. For example in the circle I'm used to casting, we call in the elementals to observe our rites. We ask them to serve us as we serve them. However we then also generate energy through magickal workings and release that energy according to our design yet we don't ask the elements to protect that energy.

I guess all I'm saying here in a nutshell is that energy just is. Magick just is. It's the way you use it that makes it negative or positive, destructive or productive. Our responsibility as Wiccan practitioners is to understand the concept of energy and do our best to use it wisely, ethically and in accordance with our construct of deity.

13th August

Robes

So what are you supposed to wear when you cast your circle? Good question! It depends on what tradition you want to follow, what your personal opinions are about circle clothing and whether your circle is for an esbat or a sabbat.

Traditionally Alexandrians and Gardnerians often go skyclad in circles. This means they are 'clad in nothing but the sky' so they're nude. That might be OK if you don't mind other folks seeing you in your birthday suit and if you feel safe doing so. However, you won't find me doing rituals wearing nothing but the skin the Goddess gave me when it's bitterly cold as it can be in an Adelaide winter or damn near roasting as it often is during an Adelaide summer! Even more, I'm not about to be eaten alive by mosquitoes either, so for me, it's robes all the way!

Personally I love the colour green and the traditional colours of Oak and Mistletoe are green and purple so that's what I choose to wear. But, if you follow the Alexandrian or Gardnerian traditions, you might wear robes relevant to the degree you've attained. As an Inclusive Wiccan, my colour choice is personal. I believe it should be for you too.

In terms of the material you make your robes from, it should be a plain colour and made from a natural fibre, perhaps wool for cool climates and cotton for warmer locations. The problem with cotton of course is that you have to iron it! So think about the

workload you might take on with the material you use. These days, many Wiccans make their robes from penne velvet because it looks nice, is very easy to throw in the washing machine and wash and never needs ironing. Alternatively, you could have lightweight robes for summer and a nice woollen cloak to go over your robes during the winter months. Patterns for robes are easily available on the internet and essentially they are just a large T shape with the top cross bar for the sleeves. Servants of the Light have a great web page you can access with both a simple and tailored pattern at
http://www.servantsofthelight.org/knowledge/makingrobes.html.

These very simple patterns are easy to cut out, even easier to sew together and can be decorated with any special embroidery that you feel suits your needs. Alternatively, you can always buy a special dress or set of clothing that you save only for ritual work. Don't forget the cords (belt) as well that you can tie round your waist. Your cords can be a length of plaited wools or cotton ropes and from those cords you can hang a small bag to hold anything you might need in circle and your athame sheath.

Popular contemporary practice encourages Wiccans to wear their robes at both esbats (full moons) and at sabbats (the festivals in the wheel of the year). Whatever colour or style of robes you choose to wear, they should be kept only for ritual work. They should be the special clothes you put on just to honour the Gods and Goddesses. They should be kept clean and well maintained so that you can feel proud to wear them before the Divine.

20th August

Some of the best Wiccan and Witchcraft websites

OK, so many of you have asked me for references to suitable books and web pages that I thought I ought to respond. In the archives of InfoCircle you'll find book references but now here comes my favourite Wiccan and Witchcraft websites. Let me say at the outset that there are a plethora of great sites (there are also some not so great) and my list will not be able to include them all so if I miss one of your favourites, please forgive me!

For learning about Wicca of course I'd have to say the obvious wouldn't I?! http://www.oakandmistletoe.com.au.

However, there are a whole bunch more websites I happily recommend to new learners. Many of these sites are also great resources when you need to show someone that you're not delving into Satanism, about to sacrifice someone's new born baby on a stone altar in the forest or turn the ex into a toad. So here goes;

http://www.religioustolerance.org/witchcra.htm
http://en.wikipedia.org/wiki/Wicca
http://wicca.timerift.net/wicca101/index.shtml
http://gamma.faithweb.com

http://www.witchvox.com/va/dt_va.html?a=ustx&c=basics&id=11793
http://www.witchonthego.com/wicca101.html
http://www.cuew.org/whatiswicca.html
http://www.ladybridget.com/w/whatwic.html
http://www.psychicmoon.co.uk/wicca_explained.htm
http://www.empathys.co.uk/1.html

For some great info on the history of Wicca, you can't go past;
http://www.geraldgardner.com/
http://www.controverscial.com/Aleister%20Crowley.htm
http://en.wikipedia.org/wiki/Aleister_Crowley

General info;
http://www.megalith.ukf.net/bigmap.htm
http://en.wikipedia.org/wik/Lunar_phase
http://www.archaeoastronomy.com/almanac.html

Hubs;
http://paganguild.gotop100.com/index.php
http://wiccaandwitchcraft.toplisted.net/index.php?id=8030
http://paganpages.org/content/

OK, so I think that's a fairly hefty list to be going on with. It's by no means exhaustive of course and in fact deosn't even contain all my favourites out it would be somewhat overwhelming if I listed every site I loved!

27th August

The Book of Shadows and how to use it

There's so much hype out there about the book of shadows (affectionately known as the BOS) that it can be quite confusing for new students to determine things like;

- What exactly is a BOS?
- What's the difference between the BOS and a diary that records nature, dreams and meditations?
- What do I put in a BOS?
- What sort of BOS am I supposed to buy or make?

Let's explain what the BOS is first and later talk through some of the hype so we can strip away the fact from the marketing. A great many Wiccans and Witches choose to have a BOS largely because it's a good way to record and keep a history of their Wiccan practice. I say "a great many" because it's not an order from above or anything so it's not a demand but it's certainly something that most practicing Witches would agree is helpful for them.

Essentially you write in your BOS all the rituals you conduct through the year, all the spell-work you might undertake and any other relevant materials that you want to keep track of. By keeping a record of all this work, you can use the same ritual or working again if you need to without hunting through a bunch of old papers and you can also check back later to see if any spell-work gave a good result or not. It would be a tragedy to do some great spell-work that delivered brilliant results but couldn't be repeated because you couldn't find a record of what you did!

Your basic circle casting ritual will probably remain the same so recording that in your BOS helps you make sure you don't drift too far from the ritual and start creating different ways to do it without realising. A case of Chinese whispers kind of thing. Your sabbats will probably be different each year so that while you celebrated Samhain in a particular way this year, next year you may feel differently and will probably want to do the ritual differently. Recording all these sabbats each time gives you an ongoing diary of what you did and also helps to give you ideas down the track when you want to create a new ritual but using some successful 'ingredients' you've used before.

So your BOS is a d ary, a ritual 'recipe' book, a grimoire and a personal collection that will become a representation of your Wiccan life journey. Many covens also have a coven BOS that records the major rituals for that group and when a seeker is initiated, traditionally they're presented with the coven book and requested to write out its contents into their own personal BOS.

So if the BOS records all that important stuff, what's the difference between that and a nature, dream and meditation diary? This is a really good question and one that continues to cause debate amongst Wiccans. Here's my take on it that not everyone will agree with but it's a practical way of explaining it.

As a new seeker, one of the important tasks you're required to attend to is writing down any significant dreams and meditations and also recording what you observe around you in nature for at least your first year and preferably much longer. Why? Because cataloguing all this helps you to see patterns in dreams and meditations that may be insights about who you are and about your connection with the Lord and Lady. Being a Wiccan and/or a Witch also means cultivating your connection and appreciation of nature so really understanding what's happening in nature helps you to get closer to it and to see how your behaviour shifts with the shifts in season. The Gods and Goddesses manifest throughout all nature so having a clear understanding about the seasons and your environment is to more clearly see the Divine.

I ask my students to keep their nature, dream and meditation diary separate for the first year from their BOS so they can focus on these topics specifically and really give them the effort they deserve. It's much easier to see patterns in all that if you don't also have to wade through records of rituals and so on. So if you keep that record separate from your BOS, it's much easier.

In addition, in my belief, a BOS becomes a sacred book that holds your personality, your dedication and your commitment to the Lord and Lady. It evolves into a wonderful collection that shows how you celebrate your faith and that's very special. With that in mind, many Wiccans and Witches spend a small fortune on beautiful leather bound or wooden covered books that are almost works of art as well as their personal ritual record. In my opinion it takes at least a year before you really work out what you want in your BOS and how you're going to record everything because it's such a personal, intimate and special book. So your first BOS can be a 'practice' one till you've worked out your system. It would be a little sad to spend lots of money on a beautiful book that you started writing in straight away and then a few months later decided you actually wanted to set it out differently. So in a nutshell, I recommend two cheap exercise books for the first year, one as your nature/dream/meditation dairy and one as your first BOS.

Speaking of your system for writing in the BOS, there are as many ways of setting up and of writing in the BOS as there are Wiccans and Witches doing it. Traditionally you should make your own tools including your BOS but not all of us are accomplished artisans so that doesn't always happen! What you can do though is buy a BOS you love and personalise it by covering it with leather yourself or painting a design on it that comes from your own creativity. You can paste bay leaves inside the cover for protection of the records inside or perhaps create a design on your computer, print that out and paste that to the front cover. Remember, this is your BOS and it should be a reflection of who you are.

Some people, me included, follow the old tradition of writing everything in their BOS by hand and while it's time consuming, there's something to be said for the wonder and power that gradually attaches itself to a well loved, hand written book. However, you could also use a ring binder and enter the pages in from a computer print out. It's much faster, much easier and you can move pages around and create sections in the binder if you want to. You could compromise as some of my students do and type the ritual up on the computer, print it out and then draw and 'scrapbook' special things onto the pages to personalise them.

I mentioned at the beginning of this article that we'd discuss the hype so let's do that now. While a BOS is a basic tool of Wicca and Witchcraft, you don't have to spend a fortune. It's not necessary. Many Wiccans one of my own teachers in fact, uses a ring binder from the local stationery shop because it's cheap, convenient and it works. She's been teaching for years, knows her stuff and after a while your BOS is going to get pretty full so a growing set of ring binders is a great way to store all the work you've done.

Wicca and its Craft s a legitimate religion with legitimate people who love and honour the Divine. There are also some wonderful artisans who create some beautiful BOS's for people and do so in love and with a sense of empathy for the religion. However, there are some people out there who make second rate quality books because it gives them an income and they don't care a toss if you pay through the nose for what might be cheap crap. Look around first, ask to look at other Wiccan's and Witch's books, look on the internet, ask at your local Pagan supplies store. In other words, get lots of information and ideas first before you spend money on a BOS system that six months later you might want to change. Your BOS should be special and one of your greatest treasures so take your time looking around. Your BOS will find you when you're ready.

3rd September

Christian versus Wiccan ritual

Recently I attended a Christian (non denominational) service as part of my ongoing belief that we should be tolerant of other religions. I'm not suggesting we have to agree with them or always attend everyone else's services but now and again I like to spread my wings and experience the spiritual rituals of other religions. Why you ask? Because it helps me affirm that I am in the right religion for me.

This particular service was run by a very good friend of mine who runs a Christian church in the middle of outback South Australia. He's a minister of a fairly 'middle of the road' denomination and he's also the visiting pastor on our remote mine site and as part of his duties he holds interfaith services for the folk working away from home with us. A fantastic man who brings people together, who ministers the Christian faith (while I minister the Pagan faith!) and who supports people as best he can. Even though I don't follow or agree with his faith, I still have immense respect for the work he does with people in outback South Australia.

What I did re-affirm for myself having attended his service though, was that I am definitely not Christian!!! I was shocked (I'm always shocked by this so you'd think I would have learnt by now wouldn't you) that the service revolved around asking the Christian God for forgiveness for my apparent sins and acknowledging what a jealous and vengeful bloke he could be when you step on the wrong side of him. I left the service astounded that anyone would want to adhere to something that made them feel like they were two years old and being told off by their Dad! Of course Mum never featured in the whole thing at all. I think she wandered off several hundred years back and left Dad to it but there ya go.

All jokes aside (and I sincerely mean no disrespect to any other religion) I genuinely think it's worthwhile attending the services of other religions so that you can really understand where your own religion sits in relation to them. If nothing else it affirms that what you believe in is right for you and it may also surprise you by offering you additional ways to look at your own practice. I've been blessed to attend rituals and services of several different religions including a variety of Wiccan and Pagan rituals in three different countries and many of them have given me ideas about ways I can connect with my Gods and Goddesses that I might otherwise have never known about. So while I might not have enjoyed getting told off by someone else's 'Dad' for stuff I personally don't think I deserved, I did learn that Wicca is my faith of choice and I'm happy right where I am!

10th September

The Wiccan obsession with 'stuff'

I recall in my early years of studying Wicca that my then High Priestess (this was several years ago) suggested that everyone in her group should all have their robes made in the same colour. Her idea was that if we all dressed in the same colour during esbat and sabbat rituals, we would feel a better connection with the community that was our coven. I found that somewhat curious given that in my novice opinion our main aim with Wicca was to forge a relationship with our idea of the Divine, not just with coven members. I wasn't quite sure how everyone having the same coloured robe, regardless of how 'cool' it might be actually fostered a deeper relationship with the Gods. But who was I to question this? I was simply an ignorant Seeker in a group of established and well trained Wiccan Priests and Priestesses.

The discussion around the need versus want of Wiccan 'stuff', those tools and artefacts we love to collect and use, abounds with views about the value of tools in contrast to the more important need to generate a relationship with the Gods and Goddesses. There appears to be a polemic argument with the voluntary (and in fact unnecessary) use of Wiccan tools at one end but with our love and passion for all things Wicca at the other. Whilst many Wiccans talk long and loud about the fact that we don't need all the paraphernalia in order to honour deity, we still go out and either buy or make a suite of tools and items that we then excuse simply as enhancing our practice.

Read almost any Pagan web page, log in to virtually any Wiccan blog or bulletin board and you will see that Wiccans adore their ritual tools. I have to admit that I love my very special tools too. There are long, explanatory lists of tools, altar items, ritual artefacts and clothing and general paraphernalia available to the Wiccan practitioner. Buck and delivers not just a list of tools but also detailed descriptions on how to make a simple ritual robe and even how to forge an athame blade.[1] Cunningham and a variety of other writers offer similar explanatory notes on Wiccan ritual items, often listing them in order of what they consider highest to lowest priority in terms of general ritual practice.[2] In my own books, I've done exactly the same thing. More often than not, the athame rates as the highest tool in terms of importance to any Wiccan followed by altar tools and ritual robes.

You don't have to dig very deep on the internet to find a plethora of web shopfronts selling all manner of items that supposedly we need to embrace our practice and that support the undercurrent of thought that in fact these tools are a necessity rather than an enhancement. Oak and Mistletoe provides a service to its students with its shop of tools as well.

Research clearly indicates that Pagans generally are well educated people but statistically earn slightly less than the average wage earner largely because they tend to migrate toward lesser paid, helping professions.[3] If this is the case, then we somehow seem to find the money to financially support the Wiccan artefact industry and as educated people we wouldn't be doing that if we didn't love our tools and paraphernalia. Moreover, research also shows that Wiccans spend proportionately more on Wiccan reading material than other minority religious practitioners.[4] We love to learn more about our religion and we love to dress up our practice with tools, with ritual items and paraphernalia and even dress ourselves in ritual robes that we somehow equate with more effective ritual practice. The real question here though is whether our love affair with all things Wiccan actually enhances or depletes our practice.

In the case of the High Priestess I introduced at the commencement of this piece and her contention that with everyone having the same coloured robes individuals would gain greater connection with the coven, this may well in fact be true. A considerable body of anthropological theory discusses how ritual and the symbols embedded within rites such as robes impart to practitioners a sense of identity and connection with the society in which that ritual takes place.[5,6] However, the role and responsibility of any religious practitioner is not just to connect with one another but to connect with deity. I doubt there's any significant research that proves that having a particular colour robe fosters a deeper relationship with one's Gods and Goddesses.

Furthermore, and rather more arguably, is it absolutely necessary for a Wiccan to have an athame given that this appears to be the most important tool according to most Wiccan writers? Gerald Gardner introduced the double edged blade as a Wiccan tool of trade along with a number of other suspect items including the controversial scourge. In addition, as a naturist he proposed working in the nude and some other rather impractical ideas as Wiccan practice. If you've ever tried to conduct a serious meditative ritual in the nude when the mosquitoes are biting or the snow is falling around you causing painful itches or frostbite, I'm sure you have wondered at the common sense of such a proposal! Just because Gerald Gardner proposed a tool or particular practice as a Wiccan inclusion, surely doesn't mean it is sacrosanct if in the same breath we argue that our main purpose is to create a relationship with the Divine.

Given as well that Wicca proposes each person has the right to develop their own relationship with deity in a way that suits them (within the basic core of Wicca of course) does that not also mean that the use of Wiccan tools is a voluntary decision, not one that is necessary? Many Wiccans will support this argument, stating that the use of any tool is simply to enhance one's ritual experience, however in practice that's not always the case. Seekers are often being taught that they really should have an athame, that they really should wear robes or go skyclad and that they need certain items on their altar in order to cast circles, conduct Wiccan ritual and in fact 'be' Wiccan. Such a claim is ludicrous. I can 'be' Wiccan without using an athame, without dressing up and without resorting to tools as props in lieu of a serious, dedicated and effective connection with deity.

The real danger here is that we may in fact end up worshipping our tools rather than worshipping our Gods. The tools become pseudo Gods as some Christian, Buddhist and other religious temples and churches have become places of awe rather than simply as venues for the worship of the Gods for whom they were built. While it's obvious that Wiccans love their tools, perhaps because they help them connect with what they perceive as being their ancestral or religious connections, what teachers must do is ensure that they teach Seekers how to honour the Gods and Goddesses without all the paraphernalia so they're equipped with the foundational aspects of Wiccan ritual practice and only then introduce tools as an adjunct rather than as inclusive, necessary tools of trade.

Having said that, some of the fallout I'm seeing now is dialogue about the guilt associated with tool use and the excuses put forward for their use. As Wiccans schooled in the foundational ritual practices of our religion, we should not need to make excuses for using tools or wearing robes or indulging in our passion for altar items of beauty and reverence. As long as we have that fundamental training and education in fostering a relationship with the Divine, then we shouldn't be swayed and cajoled into the argument that tool use is utterly unnecessary. Tool use is voluntary and when used in conjunction with sound practice and ritual work, it's appropriate and effective. The strict argument that tool use is utterly inappropriate serves little purpose other than engender within new Wiccans a confusion about the validity of tools and a guilt about using items they find beautiful as tools of honour.

I own up completely to having an extensive suite of altar tools, to having custom made robes designed especially for me, for having all the bells and whistles of a Wiccan toolkit. Furthermore I love my robes, my artefacts and my 'stuff'. I'm proud to place these items before my Gods and Goddesses as further evidence that I honour them by taking pride in how I present myself and my worship before them. I love that pre-ritual process of preparing the sacred space with particular items and preparing myself. This process 'gears up' my head for ritual work and places me in a better mental place for ritual work. But, and this is the crucial point, I didn't base my Wiccan practice on my tools but rather based my Wiccan practice on building a relationship with the Divine. I learnt how to connect with deity, with the environment, with my own inner spirit first and then used my toolkit and 'stuff' to honour and enhance that journey even further. I therefore stand proud with all my Wiccan gear and I make no excuses for indulging in my love and passion for all things Wiccan.

In conclusion then, as Wiccan teachers, it's our duty to instruct in the use of ritual tools and paraphernalia but not at the expense of the true meaning of 'being' Wiccan. As gatekeepers of Wiccan lore and practice, we must ensure that we teach Seekers how to develop and foster their relationship with the Divine as the ultimate quest and then introduce tool use as power enhancers. Moreover, teachers must enable people to adopt tool use as is their wish without associated guilt or the need to make excuses or justify why they have an expensive book of shadows because they loved it or why they chose to dress up in spider lace, black velvet cloaks with tasselled hoods or whatever. These Wiccan tools of trade should be their choice without guilt but only where they are used as voluntary, unnecessary wants rather than needs.

[1] Buckland, Ronald (1986), *Buckland's Complete Book of Witchcraft,* Llewellyn; Woodbury, Minnesota.

[2] Cunningham, Scott (2004) (1st ed. revised). *Wicca: A Guide for the Solitary Practitioner,* Llewellyn; Woodbury, Minnesota.

[3] Hume, Lynne (1997). *Witchcraft and Paganism in Australia.* Melbourne University Press; Melbourne, Australia.

[3] Rountree, Kathryn (2004). *Embracing the Witch and the Goddess: Feminist ritual-makers in New Zealand,* Routledge; London.

[4] Greenwood, Susan (2000). *Magic, Witchcraft and the Otherworld: An Anthropology,* Berg Publishers; New York.

[5] Durkheim, Emile. (1976). (2nd ed.). *The Elementary Forms of Religious Life,* Allen & Unwin; London.

[6] Geertz, Clifford. (1957). Ethos, Worldview and the Analysis of Sacred Symbols. *The Antioch Review,* 17 (4), Pp 421-437.

17th September

We don't just 'do' magick; we 'are' magick

Usually when thinking about magick, we think about how we 'do' magick but I believe we actually 'are' magick. Let me explain.

For me, magick is a universal energy which is within us, around us, is us, is everything, that everything actually is. Magick is that energy, or rather the use of that energy, to bring about an end result. Physics tells us that energy never stops, never disappears, it just changes form. You can't switch energy off and you can't switch it on because it's a constant. It may change from liquid to gas and to solid, but it also changes from thought to action or behaviour and outcome, which in turn changes to more thought and different behaviour. Energy then, just 'is'.

Stick with me as I change tack here. We usually see our own bodies as solid objects. You can't push your hand through your belly like you can slice it through the air. But here's the strange thing. Our bodies are actually energy rather than just solid objects. If we could look at our body under a huge microscope, what we'd find as we get to deeper magnifications is that our body is made up of organs, which in turn are made up of cells, which in turn are made up of atoms and so on. When you look at atoms under those massive microscopes you see that they're actually just energy, that's all they are. Atoms are vibrating energies with the neutrons and protons chasing round each other just exhibiting energy, that's it. Quantum physics identifies cells as simply the shells of continuous energy.

So if we think outside the usual square we've been told to think in for just one moment, rather than being what we thought of as solid objects, our bodies are actually pure energy. What's more, so is that tree outside, or the fish in the sea, or even this book you're holding. All those things, all that we considered to be just solid objects are in fact pure vibrating, never ending, form changing energy and if we know that magick is just the use of energy and that our bodies are pure energy, then we don't just 'do' magick, we 'are' magick. Fascinating thought isn't it?

24th September

Spring Equinox/Ostar/Eostre

A Lesser Sabbat and a Sun Quarter Day
Northern Hemisphere March 21st
Southern Hemisphere September 21st
Seasonal Relevancy
Spring has arrived and there's an equal balance of light and dark. The flowers are all blooming again, the birds are nesting and getting ready for their young and all around, new life is bursting forth in a new generation of animals and plants.

Mythological Relevancy
This sabbat is named after the Saxon Goddess Ostara and this festival specifically marks an equal balance between male and female energies which coincides perfectly with the fact that the days and nights are of equal length. Thus there is spiritual balance in all things. The young Oak King, who's grown to a young man, now courts the maiden Goddess.

Popular Traditions
Eggs are symbolic of new life and Wiccans use painted eggs to celebrate the wonderful eruption of new life all around

them. Throw hard boiled, painted eggs high into the sky and as you do make a wish for the summer months ahead. The higher the egg goes, the more likely your wish will come true. Bury the fallen eggs to cement your wish. Bake and eat Hot Cross Buns marked with an equilateral cross to symbolise all things equal.

A Contemporary Spring Equinox- Ostara Ritual

Hold the ritual in a park or open garden area. Decorate the altar with bright yellow daffodils and other spring flowers. Mark the perimeter of the circle with spring flowers. On the altar have;

- Yellow card cut into the shape of big sunflowers with petal sections that can eventually fold up so that the flower shape becomes a bowl (1 sunflower for each person present).
- A pen for each person to use.
- A pot of parrot or bird seed.

Cast the circle as normal if there are no visitors present, otherwise, omit the circle casting.

The ritual leader says to the group "the spring equinox is a both a time of balance and a time of renewal. It is a time of balance because this event marks one of two points in the year when the days are the same length as the nights. Thus there is balance in light and darkness".

"It is also a time of renewal and rebirth as spring provides the warmth and light for new plants to grow, for young animals to grow healthy and fit, and for life to blossom around us. So as the caretakers of our precious planet and as the architects of our own life balance and renewal, we can use this time to refocus on those things that are important to us."

Give each person a sunflower card and a pen saying "each of you now have before you a symbolic sunflower, one of the flowers that erupts at this time of year and grows toward full bloom in the summer. Take a few moments now to consider what parts of your life are out of balance. Are you spending too much time and too much effort on one part of your life at the expense of other, equally or more important parts? Are you spending too much time on things and not on people? Do you use one set of behaviours instead of spreading your wings and trying better ways to cope? Are you ignoring parts of your life, parts of who you are when you should be balancing your life and being a whole person?"

"When you are ready, take your pen and write in the centre of your sunflower one way you will rebalance your life. Write down one behaviour or one aspect of your life you will change to bring your life back into balance."

"Now take your sunflower and bend the petals up so that you form a bowl with your committed behaviour change written inside."

When all participants have done this, have someone take the pot of bird seed and pour some seed into each of the sunflower bowls. The ritual leader then says "your commitments to rebalance your lives are now nestled beneath seed, which is the icon of new life, of rebirth and of renewal. Please take your sunflower bowls home. Each bowl signifies both life balance and rebirth. At home, place your bowl out in the garden to feed the local birds and to give to the Earth your commitment to rebalance your life."

Consecrate and then have the cakes and ale, then close the circle. Follow up with a feast.

1st October

Discrimination of non Christian faiths

I'm a pretty liberal person. "Live and let live" I say and I don't care if someone is black, white, green with red spots, old, young, intelligent, poor, likes steak and kidney pudding or has a pet poodle. I don't care if they're Christian, Wiccan, Buddhist or even believe that pigs will fly. But I do care if they don't allow me or others to follow a chosen faith no matter how obscure, unusual or socially misunderstood.

A few years back my daughter was enrolled in an otherwise great school with great teachers and equally as great kids. The curriculum was wonderful, the teaching quality without question and she was very happy there. Only one thing irked me. They had a policy that allowed all kids to wear a necklace with a cross on it (Australia like the UK and the USA is a Christian based country) but the kids had to provide a written letter from their parents if they wanted to wear any other jewellery like decorative earrings or perhaps a necklace with a locket on it. The idea was to ensure that kids didn't come to school wearing dangerously long, dangly earrings or knuckle duster rings or so on. What's wrong with that you ask? Nothing,... if you're a Christian kid.

That policy meant that coming from a Wiccan family, my daughter had to provide a letter from me saying I gave her permission to wear her much loved pentacle necklace. The Jewish kids had to provide a letter of permission to wear their religious jewellery and so on. Where does it end? Do the Sikh kids need to do the same for their turbans? What about the Muslim girls and the Jilbat?

Hopefully we're becoming more tolerant of others and maybe moving much more toward the 'live and let live' approach and that's great. But many of us are responsible for the development, or indeed the modification, of policies in the workplace, in our social clubs and sporting groups, and in the approaches of our families and so on that enable people of all religions to have freedom to follow their path without prejudice or harassment. It's our duty as Wiccans and simply as world citizens to make sure we foster greater appreciation and acceptance of the right for everyone to follow their faith as long is it doesn't harm others. Wanting freedom to practice Wicca goes both ways. As we demand respect for the right to follow our Wiccan path, we must also demand the right for everyone to follow their own religion as well. Live and let live is a right for everyone even if they do think pigs will fly.

8th October

3 steps to easy visualisation

OK, so visualisation isn't always an easy skill for the beginner to get to grips with, that's true, but there are some simple tricks and tips that can help you become a visualisation expert faster and easier. Let's just make sure you understand first though exactly why visualisation is so important.

After the ethics and basic fundamentals, visualisation is probably THE single most important tool in your Wiccan and Witchcraft armoury. It's the technique you'll use eventually to cast circles, to create magickal workings and to connect with the Divine. It's your pathway to Wiccan and Craft success in other words and so it's incredibly important to master as soon as you can. So what's some easy ways to help the process?

Step 1

Relax! Simple as that, just slow down, don't put so much pressure on yourself to *achieve* visualisation and have some fun with it. It's not a competition and you don't have to be an expert in four days. It can take years and years of practice to become adept at full visualisation so don't expect miracles for several weeks or even months. Give yourself permission to not get it right and perfect for a while!

Step 2

If it's hard to see things at first, cheat. Instead of trying to create things in your mind to see, remember recent things instead. It's far easier to see an image in your mind if you already know what it looks like so if you're being asked to remember a meal, an animal, a face or whatever, remember one from this morning or from yesterday. If your Craft teacher is telling you to visualise a face or a meal, then think about your friend's face who you saw yesterday or what you had for breakfast this morning. See how much easier it is to see a picture of something in your mind when you already know what it looks like? Spend a few days practicing that first so you begin to feel comfortable with the process of opening your mind up to memories and seeing them again in your mind's eye.

When you're ready, try and remember a face you saw or a meal you ate or the dog from next door that you haven't seen for at least a week. Stretch out that time frame so that instead of remembering something from a few hours ago, you're now remembering something from several days ago. Then stretch that out even further and try and remember a face from many years ago or how it felt to eat your favourite food when you were a child. Really test your memory and get your mind's eye to remember things from many years previously.

Step 3

Now that you've got your mind's eye working to visualise things from your distant memory, it's time to use your imagination and create pictures in your mind of things that haven't happened yet or that you want to happen. That's real visualisation for Wiccan and Witchcraft purposes and is what you should eventually be aiming for.

Casting circles and creating magical workings is all about using your imagination to focus your visualisation techniques so that you eventually create representations of your visualisations on other planes. Play at this point with your imagination and create rooms complete with furniture. Imagine what your favourite room would look like if money was no object. Imagine your ideal home, ideal car, holiday, partner. Really have fun with your imagination and draw pictures in your mind of what you'd like.

When you design these rooms, houses, cars or whatever, try and hear what the people say, smell the fragrances of the room, feel the temperatures. Use all your senses as you imagine and create because these skills are the exact same skills that you need for Wiccan visualisations. By the time you can achieve these outcomes, you'll be a master visualiser!

15th October

Why I get up every morning

This morning I received a really inspiring email from a very dear work colleague, Alistair, which I'd like to share with you. It simply had the words "Why I get up every morning" in the subject header and attached was a photo of Alistair with his toddler daughter. It brought tears to my eyes. Let me put this in context for you.

I work in the mining industry and each one of us spends at least one week away in every two at our site in a remote location. We literally work in the desert almost a 1000 kilometres away from the nearest city, away from our families, away from our loved ones, away from our friends, our homes, our pets, the supermarket, the bank, the local sports club, the hairdresser, the gym, the coffee shop and so on. We work in what I call a 'dissociated environment' and while we've created a community here together at our site, it's nowhere near the same as being home with the people we love.

Alistair's email drove home for me just how incredibly important our loved ones are. Sure we might get annoyed when the kids whinge and whine about not having the same clothes or toys as their friends at school, and of course we sometimes get frustrated when our partner's drive us nuts, but we're human and so are they. Stop for just one minute right now and ask yourself these questions. What impact would it have on your life if you never saw those kids again? How would you cope with never hearing their laughter or feeling their trusting hand in yours? How would your life change if your frustrating but devoted partner never came home again? Where would your joy, your satisfaction, and your peace come from if you could never feel the touch of your loved one again or see their smile?

People, our children our parents, our partners, our loved ones are always what present us with the most frustrating challenges but that's because they're so dam important. If they weren't important to us, we wouldn't care. But we do care and sometimes we forget that we care. We can own all the 'shiny things' in the world like the latest toaster, the fastest production car, the biggest house and so on and while we might own things, we still may not be at peace. We will never own our loved ones but they are the treasures we have the privilege to share our lives with every day. Our loved ones are the most precious, the most valuable and important impacts on our lives and if you stop for just one moment and think about how your life would change if they were no longer in it, you can quickly see that the toaster, the car and the house mean nothing in comparison.

So today, tomorrow, the day after that and the day after that, wake up giving thanks for the treasures of your life. Not the 'shiny things' but your loved ones. Today, tomorrow, the day after that and the day after that let your treasures know just how valuable they really are to you. Make sure they know that they're the most important treasure in your world because that's exactly what they are. They're your 'shiny treasure'.

22nd October

The differences in the southern and northern wheel of the year

The wheel of the year is an important construct in Wiccan practice and it's the liturgical calendar for our religion. However, while sticking to the original dates for the northern hemisphere folks is easy, the real problems come about for the southern hemisphere practitioners. Depending on where you live and your approach to your own, personalised practice, the dates for each of the wheel's celebrations may well be different. We've thus defaulted as a global Wiccan community into three main groups.

- Those who stick to, and follow, the northern hemisphere wheel of the year because they live there, because it's simpler, or because they don't know what else to do.
- Those who follow a completely revised southern wheel of the year which essentially is the opposite of the northern one.
- Those who follow a more organic calendar based on their local geography and ecology.

Now let me say at this point that none of these approaches are wrong and as a practitioner of a religion that expects you to take responsibility for your practice, it's up to you to determine what will work for you. So many people are modifying their wheel of the year to reflect their own ecology and for many practitioners this has enabled them to feel much more in tune with their own, local natural world rather than one imposed on them by others.

It's also not just as simple of swapping the seasons over either, oh that it was that easy! For example, the weather patterns in large continents like Australia and the Americas dictate that during summer, in some places it can be extremely hot and yet in others in the same country it can be quite mild. Alaska has a different summer weather pattern than does California. In Australia, Tasmania has a mild summer while Darwin suffers under oppressive heat in summer. So even in the same country, the weather patterns can be quite different.

To make matters even more complicated, while the northern wheel of the year says that summer is the time of life and natural abundance, in those very hot places rather than being the time of year when plant and animal life is thriving as it would be in the homeland of this religion we call Wicca, life is hibernating from the extreme heat. In the summers in the Nevada Desert in the USA and the Simpson Desert in Australia, plants are not growing gaily, harvests are not ripening and young animals and birds are not taking their first tentative steps or flights into the big wide world. So many Wiccan practitioners shy away from celebrating harvest festivals for instance and instead modify them to reflect what's actually happening in their ecology. What's the point in celebrating a harvest festival of summer when all the plant life is dried up, shrivelled or hibernating!

While all this is true, and indeed is an ever present problem for both northern and southern hemisphere Wiccans, we do have to follow something related to our wheel of the year or we wouldn't be Wiccans anymore. I mean for example, if the Christians decided that Christmas didn't fit anymore and they removed it entirely, it would probably be a big dent in the Christian liturgical calendar! So, I've offered here the two more traditional wheels of the year (northern and southern) so you at least have a framework from which to work. I'd encourage you to develop your own liturgical calendar if your local ecology doesn't reflect either wheel appropriately until you come up with something that suits your needs but remember always that the natural cycle of life around us probably needs to be hardwired into the God and Goddess stories in order to weld it within the Wiccan faith. We are after all celebrating a religion and without those mythical stories, you're just celebrating nature, even if she is glorious in her own right.

Northern (and Original) Wiccan Wheel of the Year
2nd February - Imbolg (also known as Candlemas)
21st March - Spring Equinox (also known as Ostara)
30th April - Beltaine
22nd June - Summer Solstice (also known as Midsummer)
31st July – Lughnasadh (also known as Lammas)
21st September – Autumn Equinox (also known as Mabon)
31st October – Samhain (also known as All Hallows Eve)
22nd December - Winter Solstice (also known as Yule)

Southern Wiccan Wheel of the Year
2nd February - Lughnasadh (also known as Lammas)
21st March - Autumn Equinox (also known as Mabon)
30th April - Samhain (also known as All Hallows Eve)
22nd June - Winter Solstice (also known as Yule)
31st July – Lughnasadh (also known as Lammas)
21st September – Spring Equinox (also known as Ostara)
31st October – Beltaine
22nd December - Summer Solstice (also known as Midsummer)

29th October

Beltaine

A Greater Sabbat and an Earth Cross-Quarter Day
Northern Hemisphere April 30th
Southern Hemisphere October 31st
Seasonal Relevancy
   The summer begins at this point and the days are warm and balmy. The nights are getting shorter and growth is all around.

Mythological Relevancy
   This is a time of great fertility and is a fun filled time in marked contrast to the sober and sombre sabbat of Samhain. It celebrates the sacred marriage of the Oak King and the Goddess and the consummation of that union. The fire God Baal is celebrated at this time as the God of light or 'The Bright One' while the Goddess Maya is also celebrated.

Popular Traditions
   This is a true fertility festival with dancing round the maypole (an ancient phallic symbol) to symbolise the sexual union between male and female energies.
   Light a balefire with nine different types of wood (three pieces of each wood type) for the God Baal. Leap over the purifying flames and let them cleanse you of unwanted

behaviours or openly state your desire and as you jump, let the flames take those desires to the skies to be fulfilled.

A Contemporary Beltaine Ritual

Decorate the perimeter of the circle with flowers. A maypole should be set up in the east quarter with ribbons tied to it at the top. There should be at least one ribbon for each person present. There should be a balefire set in the north quarter. This should be a festival of fun, frivolity, dancing and laughter. It is not a sombre affair at all.

Cast the circle as normal if there are no visitors present, otherwise, omit the circle casting. A covener shouts "haste, haste! No time to wait! We're off to the sabbat, so don't be late!" The ritual leader shouts "to the sabbat!" and everyone shouts "to the sabbat!"

The ritual leader leads the coveners in a dance around the circle with everyone singing and chanting. The music of "The Lord of the Dance" is particularly good for this especially using the following words adapted from the original lyrics of Sydney B Carter by Spiral Child.

She danced on the water, and the wind was Her horn.
The Lady laughed, and everything was born,
and when She lit the sun and its light gave Him birth,
the Lord of the Dance first appeared on the Earth.

(Chorus): Dance, dance, where ever you may be,
I am the Lord of the Dance, you see!
I live in you, and you live in Me,
and I lead you all in the Dance, said He!

I danced in the morning when the world was begun,
I danced in the moon and the stars and the sun.
I was called from the darkness by the song of the Earth,
I joined in the song, and She gave Me the birth!

I dance in the circle when the flames leap up high,
I dance in the fire, and I never, ever, die.
I dance in the waves of the bright summer sea,
for I am the Lord of the wave's mystery.

I sleep in the kernel, and dance in the rain,
I dance in the wind, and thru the waving grain,
and when you cut me down, I care nothing for the pain.
In the spring I'm the Lord of the Dance once again!

I dance at the sabbat when you dance out the spell,
I dance and sing that everyone be well,
and when the dancing's over do not think that I am gone,
to live is to dance! So I dance on, and on!

I see the maidens laughing as they dance in the sun,
and I count the fruits of the harvest, one by one.
I know the storm is coming, but the grain is all stored,
so I sing of the dance of the Lady, and Her Lord.

The horn of the Lady cast its sound 'cross the plain,
the birds took the notes, and gave them back again,
till the sound of Her music was a song in the sky,
and to that song there is only one reply.

The moon in her phases, and the tides of the sea,
the movement of the Earth, and the seasons that will be,
are the rhythm for the dancing, and a promise thru the years,
that the dance goes on thru all our joy, and tears.

We dance ever slower as the leaves fall and spin,
and the sound of the horn is the wailing of the wind.
The Earth is wrapped in stillness, and we move in a trance,
but we hold on fast to our faith in the dance!

The sun is in the southland and the days grow chill,
and the sound of the horn is fading on the hill.
'Tis the horn of the Hunter, as he rides across the plain,
and the Lady sleeps 'till the spring comes again.

The sun is in the southland and the days lengthen fast,
and soon we will sing for the winter that is past.
Now we light the candles and rejoice as they burn,
and we dance the dance of the sun's return!

They danced in the darkness and they danced in the night.
They danced on the Earth, and everything was light.
They danced out the darkness and they danced in the dawn,
and the day of that dancing is still going on!

I gaze on the heavens and I gaze on the Earth,
and I feel the pain of dying, and re-birth,
and I lift my head in gladness, and in praise,
for the dance of the Lord, and His Lady gay.

I dance in the stars as they whirl throughout space,
and I dance in the pulse of the veins in your face.
No dance is too great, no dance is too small.
You can look anywhere, for I dance in them all!

Everyone gathers around the maypole and takes a ribbon. The ritual leader says "Beltaine is a time of fertility. The maypole and ribbons symbolise the sacred union between male and female and the creation of new life for the year ahead." Everyone then dances around the pole holding their ribbons, intertwining them as they go until they are all tied around the pole.

Everyone then moves to the north quarter where the balefire is set and burning. The maiden says "jumping the balefire is an old fertility tradition often done together by couples who would like to be blessed with the seed and creation of children. For those of you who have a beloved partner, the balefire wish is often one of long lived health and happiness in your sacred union together. Today we honour the Lord and Lady with our rite and ask that they bestow upon us their blessings for fertility, perhaps not of children, but of good luck and happiness. I invite you all now to jump the balefire and send your wishes for good fortune up to the Lord and Lady in the rising smoke from this balefire. Consider your good luck wish, offer it to the rising smoke and set it with your jump!"

Everyone has as many turns at jumping the balefire as they wish. Couples can jump together if they wish to honour their marriage. Consecrate and then have the cakes and ale then close the circle. Follow up with a feast.

5th November

Patron and matron deities

We all know that Wicca is a polytheistic religion which in a nutshell means that its practitioners honour a number of different Gods and Goddesses rather than a single deity. But while many Wiccans practice this way, they may also have a patron God and a matron Goddess who are their 'special', or without meaning to sound flippant, 'pet' God and Goddess. They will often honour these two deities in regular rituals and will dedicate many other workings to them. Many covens are named after a particular God or Goddess who becomes the Divine icon of that group.
    It's a great thing to have a special God and Goddess that you can create a much deeper, more personal relationship with but it's not necessary and many Wiccans are happy to share their love across a range of deities and indeed a range of pantheons. One of the dangers with having patron and matron deities is that you can slip into duotheism instead of polytheism without even realising it. In other words, you just end up honouring one God and one Goddess and forget that our religion is actually one that honours a great may deities. So by all means have a patron God and a matron Goddess, but don't forget the other equally as wonderful deities around and within us.
    I'm often asked "how do I know who my matron Goddess is and my patron God?" This simple answer is that when the time is right, they will make themselves known to you. Don't force it, let it

happen. It may be that one day a thought or sign will come to you, maybe followed a few days later by another. Gradually you'll get to realise that someone is talking to you directing you their way. Or alternatively, it may be that a God or Goddess does a whammy and just hits you with their presence and it's blatantly obvious that you belong with them. Whatever way they make themselves known to you, let it happen. As they say, when the student is ready, the teacher will come.

12th November

We learn Wicca and Witchcraft with our soul as well as our brain

One of the things that's always fascinated me is how we learn to become Wiccans and Witches. I don't mean reading books on Wicca or conducting rituals. That's *head* or *brain* stuff. I mean how we *become* Wiccans with our heart, our cells and our very souls.

Trying to be humble here, I finished a PhD research topic in 2008 in which I researched how Wiccans and Witches learn to be Wiccans and Witches and the very clear result was that we learn with more than our heads; we learn with our souls.[1,2] Academia has argued up until recently that all adults learn in three major ways, cognitively (brains and heads), behaviourally (hands and behaviours) and in a humanistic fashion (with our whole beings) but none of them considered that adults also learn with their intuition or with their souls.

Think about a time when you heard the phone ring or the door bell chime and you instinctively knew who was ringing or visiting you. Maybe think about a time when you had a premonition that something was going to happen and whamo, it happened. How did you learn to do that? Did you read a book that taught you how to do it? I don't think so. Did you take a class at college, "Premonitions 101", read a text book, write an essay or two and complete and exam? Probably not. The chances are that this skill developed, or more likely was present at birth, got squashed as you went through childhood and then slowly developed again when you gave it credence and supported it. But you probably didn't use your brain to learn it by reading a book. I'd suggest you learnt it instinctively with your soul.

My research showed that when learning how to do ritual for example, Wiccans and Witches learnt to *feel* ritual as much as they learnt about how to do the ritual. In other words, there was brain stuff that taught us to use candles, to do this bit before that bit and so on, but we also learn to *feel* or *sense* the ritual, and we did so with our intuition and soul. The research also showed that when we first experienced these feelings, we very often poo-poohed them thinking we'd auto suggested it, made it up or something like that. We had to have several events where what we felt, the premonitions we had, the messages we received from deity were confirmed by events that actually occurred later on. In other words, we learnt with our instinct or soul, then we had to have that learning affirmed so we believed we could do it and then we went full steam into learning more.

For me, this was fascinating because my job as an HR and Training Manager means I develop learning programs and systems for adults. It was wonderful to think that instead of just curriculums, systems, essays, tests, competencies and all the red tape of adult education, I could actually teach and engage with students through their hearts, through their instincts, through their soul.

So next time you have a premonition or you *feel* and *sense* a ritual, know that you're on the right track. Learning with your soul is now as credible as learning with your brain.

[1] Smith, Zena (Ziggy) (2009), *How and What Witches Learn: Modern Witchcraft in Suburban Australia,* Covenstead Press; Buffalo, New York.

[2] Smith, Zena (Ziggy) (2009), *How and What Witches Learn: Modern Witchcraft in Suburban Australia,* Oak and Mistletoe; South Australia.

19th November

Free access to Wiccan information and training

One of my pet peeves is this continuing conversation (or battle depending on who you talk to) within the Wiccan community about access to quality Wiccan information and training for potential students. Depending on the tradition (and indeed the coven leadership on many occasions), there seems to be this notion that Wiccan training is only available to people who meet certain criteria such as students *must*;

- Be taught face to face.
- Reach a minimum standard of literacy before they're let in.
- do Tarot or Runes or whatever other favourite divination method is flavour of the month
- Pay squillions of dollars or pounds before they get any information (particular screaming of horror at that one!)
- Attend *every* sabbat forever and a day to remain a part of the coven.
- Wear whatever they're told, or not to, at rituals.
- Be white, middle class people with good educations and jobs before teaching is available.

Look, much as I know this will annoy a number of people (including some of my own readership I suspect) in my opinion, everyone has the right to information about Wicca and it doesn't matter whether they're white, black or dayglo green with pink spots. It doesn't matter if they are geographically isolated and simply can't get to every coven meeting, it doesn't matter if they have caring responsibilities and the needs of their kids/parents/pets frequently have to come before coven related business. Everyone has the right to knowledge; good quality, ethical, appropriate knowledge and I don't care what their circumstances are, everyone has that right.

In terms of training, that's different than information. While I believe that everyone has the absolute right to access top quality Wiccan information at any time, I also believe that everyone (regardless of their colour, location or circumstances) also has the right to *access* training. (That will really stir up the battle I suspect!)

Let's clarify something here, I said that everyone has the right to *access* training, regardless of whether they can attend every time or not, whether they have caring responsibilities, whether they have no car and are 400 kilometres away from a group or whatever. *Everyone* has the right to access both good quality information and good quality teaching. So online teaching like that from Oak and Mistletoe and like that from the one or two other great quality online teaching schools is a brilliant way for socially or geographically isolated people to access that information and training.

But, and here's the big but, while everyone has the right to access Wiccan information and training, those people accessing that training also have the responsibility to do their part and actually engage with it. A teacher doesn't do training 'to' the student, they do training 'with' the student. So training is a two way street with joint responsibility and joint effort. Your teacher puts in the effort to teach so the student needs to put in the effort to learn.

That learning though can take place online, face to face, through reading, through research, through watching, and of course always through practicing. Wicca is a 'doing' religion and the training is about 'doing' it as well as 'knowing' about it. That's where the student's responsibility comes into play.

I may be one of those 'neo-Wiccans' that the Wiccan traditionalists despise but sobeit. I was taught the old way and then initiated within another, different oath bound coven before I moved into a more contemporary version of our religion and while I absolutely uphold the value of that teaching methodology, there are also other, equally as valid and robust forms of teaching our wonderful religion. What I get annoyed about is the sublime hierarchy, the blatant discrimination and the absolute snobbery around teaching where some people will tell you that you're not a true Wiccan unless you were taught by an initiated Wiccan within the confines of an oath bound coven. What utter claptrap!

If you are a Wiccan student, eager to learn about Wicca but not able, or prepared, to do so within a coven, then you still have *every* right to top quality, ethical Wiccan knowledge and training and don't you ever forget that your needs as a student are equally, if not more, important than the dogma and restrictions of some traditions and teachers.

We're living in the 21st century, not in the dim dark ages of post war England when Wicca was first developed. I've been teaching adults now as a profession vocationally for more than 25 years and teaching and training always has to be centred round the student, not around the teacher or the topic. So students and people new to Wicca, you stand up for your rights because you might be a beginner in Wicca but you're still an adult and you do have the right to good quality, ethical information and training. Don't you ever let anyone tell you otherwise!

26th November

How covens are structured

While students learning in a face to face coven quickly begin to understand how their coven is structured and who does what, it's not so easy for solitary students. They don't get the benefit of regular exposure to the activates of a working coven and so the roles of coven members and its hierarchy can seem like a mystery. It's really not that difficult actually and depending on the tradition and customs of the coven there are a variety of ways it can be structured

The more traditional covens, which follow the older style of Wicca, tend to remain within the more time-honoured framework and have what's called an Inner and Outer Court. Think of a picture of a shooting target with its rings. The outside, perimeter circle includes the Outer Court. Students who are learning the ropes and who've not been initiated yet. It's common practice for members of the Outer Court not to be invited to full moon esbats or in fact any ritual with the exception of perhaps sabbats, so they're role is to purely learn and develop enough understanding prior to seeking initiation. During that time in Outer Court (traditionally at least a year and a day), the Inner Court members and the High Priestess has time to 'size the student up' and see whether they have the potential skills and personality and energy fit to match their existing coven dynamics.

Once the student has been initiated into that coven however, they move one ring closer to centre of our target circle and join the Inner Court. Immediately after initiation, they are First Degrees and will remain so until they are initiated into a higher degree. Whilst at this level, they learn how to cast basic circles, they develop a deeper appreciation for magick, they learn much more about the sabbats and the wheel of the year and gradually increase and mesh their circle skills with their coven brothers and sisters. Generally speaking a First Degree must spend at least a year at that level before they can seek initiation to the next level. They must be proficient at circle casting and have an acceptable level of general skills before they can move forward.

Having been accepted and undertaken the Second Degree initiation, the Inner Court member is then a Second Degree and their training and responsibility intensifies significantly. They will now be expected to share responsibility for teaching the Outer Courters and even the First Degrees, they will probably take on specific roles within the coven such as the Man in Black, the Scribe or the Maiden and they will be heavily involved in the design and development of coven rituals and planning. Many Second Degrees will remain at that level for a decade or more before being invited to take the Third Degree initiation and this is deliberately so they can gain serious expertise in the management of a coven as well as in Wiccan practice.

The Third Degree initiation is the only initiation which cannot be asked for by the practitioner. The First and Second Degree initiations are never offered to someone but instead must be actively sought by the practitioner themselves. The Third Degree initiation however is different and is only given to a Second Degree when the High Priestess considers that person is skilled and ready to lead their own coven. It's bad manners for a Second Degree to ask for the Third Degree initiation. While this is based on convention, the fact remains that the newly initiated Third Degree is expected to hive off and form their own coven and occasionally they will take some of the mother coven practitioners with them. Hence the need to be very careful when considering this level of initiation.

While the structure above is the more traditional concept, there are also a growing number of covens and traditions which have a more flexible approach to their hierarchy and structure. Many covens now employ a more democratic approach and have elected High Priestesses and High Priests and coven roles. They may have a system where the roles are shared across the more senior members or rotated. The three degree system may be flattened to a single level or there may be simply students and members. There may also be Friends of the Coven who are neither members nor students but folk who share sabbats and special occasions with the coven.

So the structure of a coven is often dependent on both the tradition and the approach of the coven leadership. There are so many varieties now and there are strengths and weaknesses with them all. The key is to consider what structure and expectations may work for you before committing to any coven.

3rd December

Which books are great for newcomers to Wicca?

One of the first questions people interested in Wicca often ask is "what books should I read?" Good question because it depends very much on which tradition you're interested in and if you're learning with a group, what books they recommend. There's a tonne of books out there and the pile is growing by the day as authors jump on the bandwagon and publish their own version of Wicca. The books also range across a huge (and constantly growing) plethora of topics and sadly focus much more on the *how to do it* kind of approach rather than the *why I should do it* fundamentals. To illustrate this, head off to your local bookshop and browse the array of 'New Age' books. You'll see that very few of them focus on the underpinning religion of Wicca and instead they tend to fall into these type of categories;

- The 101 'how to' type books,
- Divination like runes, tarot, numerology etc.,
- Dream interpretation,
- Mythologies of the world,
- Recipes and scripts for conducting rituals.

It saddens me that many authors have focused on the commercial 'fluffy bunny, how to do it' end of the market and have shied away from the serious end of Wicca which is the explanation and exploration of Wicca as a contemporary, polytheistic religion. But anyway...

For the very new beginner who's still exploring what it's all about, you can't go past these books;

- Treleven, Amethyst (2008). *The Seekers Guide to Learning Wicca: Training to First Degree for the Southern Hemisphere.* Oak and Mistletoe; South Australia.
- Treleven, Amethyst (2008). *The Seekers Guide to Learning Wicca: Training to First Degree for the Northern Hemisphere.* Oak and Mistletoe: South Australia.
- Cunningham, Scott (2002). *Wicca: A Guide for the Solitary Practitioner* (1st ed. revised). Llewellyn Publications; St Paul, Minnesota.
- Buckland, Raymond (1986). *Buckland's Complete Book of Witchcraft* (2nd ed.). Llewellyn Publications; St Paul, Minnesota..
- Sabin, Thea (2006). *Fundamentals of Philosophy & Practice: Wicca for Beginners.* Llewellyn Publications; Woodbury, Minnesota.

The list looks like an advertisement for Llewellyn doesn't it but the fact is, they are the global leader in commercial Pagan related materials (and no I don't get a commission!) These titles are staple beginners' books with ethical, sensible information and guidance. While my own books focus on Inclusive Wicca and Raymond Buckland's book is really based on Saxon Wicca, they all provide the reader with a broad, down to earth explanation of the fundamental underpinnings of Wicca as well as giving introductory information on how to give it a go and *do it*.

For a little more in-depth reading, I'd also suggest you read;

- MacMorgan, Kaatryn (2006). *All One Wicca.* Covenstead Press; Buffalo, New York.
- Farrar, Janet & Stewart (1981) *A Witches' Bible: The Complete Witches Handbook.* Robert Hale Publishers; Kent, United Kingdom.

"All One Wicca" explores Wicca in a little more depth than some of the other titles and provides an alternative teaching program for eclectic Wicca. By comparison, "The Witches' Bible" is a great read that shows how the more traditionalist Alexandrian approach is practiced. While this tradition is much older than contemporary Wicca, the book is a fabulous doorway into the history of current practice. Happy reading!

10th December

Wiccan magick meets "The Secret"

I've been reading "The Secret" by Rhonda Byrne[1] and as I read through her pages it occurred to me that what Rhonda describes as the law of attraction is in fact the same as what we'd describe as sympathetic magick. I'd agree with critics who may say that there are some things in an ethical, Wiccan magickal context that the practitioner wouldn't seek to attract to themselves (that's a whole other article) but essentially the principles Rhonda espouses are extraordinarily similar to those Wiccans would argue are magick.

The Secret suggests that 'like attracts like' and that whatever it is you actively seek and believe will come to you, does in fact materialise (good and bad). Even given the ethical constraints of sympathetic and attraction magick, I'd have to admit that this sounds remarkably similar to our own construct of attraction magick. I'd argue that in conducting spell-work to attract things to ourselves such as happiness, money, health, a new home or whatever it may be, we put in place the forces of natural energy that bring about our desired result. While we might use additional items in that spell-work such as candles, oils, herbs, poppets or whatever that Rhonda doesn't include, essentially we're using our minds to instruct and direct universal energy so that it develops into our chosen outcome exactly as Rhonda Byrne describes.

That lead me to think about what other authors have also said about creating your own desired future. There are several famous authors and motivational speakers such as Zig Ziglar, Anthony Robbins, Robert Kiyosaki and so on, who have shouted long and hard to the world that each person is the sole creator and architect of their own lives. While they may use different labels for their approach (Anthony Robbins uses NLP for instance), they're pretty much all saying the same as many Wiccans say. You are your life's architect. What's more, you're also responsible for the outcome. So if you're life is one you're happy with, that's to your credit. If your life is not what you wanted, that's something you have to look at and openly explore how you got where you are.

The Law of Return clearly says that we get back what we put out and if we take a look at that construct from the inside, then that also means that whatever we thought about ourselves, whatever we decided with our self talk was about who we are, then that's exactly who we now are. Each one of us has an idea in our heads about who we are, what attributes and issues we have and where we want to be. The challenge is threefold. The first is to make that view of ourselves the very best it can be, the second is to make it so and the third is to know we're responsible for our own life outcomes as a result.

[1] Byrne, Rhonda (2006). *The Secret,* Beyond Words Publishing; Oregon.

17th December

Summer Solstice/Midsummer's Eve/Litha

A Lesser Sabbat and a Sun Quarter Day
Northern Hemisphere June 21st
Southern Hemisphere December 21st
Seasonal Relevancy

Litha marks the longest day of the year and the zenith of summer. The sun blazes down, the ground below us holds its heat, the grass is rampant and the baby birds are now flying on their own.

Mythological Relevancy

The Holly King is born of the Goddess and the Oak King (his father) dies. This symbolic cycle is repeated each year as new life takes over from old.

In synopsis, the King marries the Goddess (who is his mother) fathers his own child, then dies in sacrifice so that his son might take over.

Popular Traditions

With the sun at its zenith, this is traditionally the time when magic is at its full strength. Many rituals incorporate some form of magic at this time.

Because the sun has reached its peak and will be slowly growing dim from this point on, this is also a great time of year for banishing magic. Banish away the behaviours or the issues and situations you have that no longer serve you. Rid yourself of aspects of your life that bring you down rather than support you.

A Contemporary Summer Solstice - Litha Ritual

Decorate the altar and mark the circle perimeter with summer flowers. Have on the altar a prepared daisy (or other weed) chain, an orange candle and some bergamot oil. Have a cauldron in the centre of the circle. Ideally this ritual should be conducted at midday on the year's longest day. Cast the circle as normal if there are no visitors present, otherwise, omit the circle casting.

The ritual leader moves to the south and says "we gather here before you, the blazing God of summer's sun, to honour you and bathe under the strength and light that is yours. The wheel of the year is turning again, as it does year after year. From the time of Yule when you were reborn of the Goddess, through Ostara you grew and now you light the days with the magnificence of your full strength. Tomorrow we will see you slowly wane toward the autumn equinox only to once again be sacrificed to the darkness of winter. But as the wheel of the year turns, we know you will always return to us. As you blaze in the skies before us now, may our lives blaze in glory below."

The ritual leader dresses the candle with the bergamot oil saying "as the zenith of the sun God's power reaches its height so too does our magickal will and intent. And as the sun God's power wanes from this point, so too do our misfortunes. I infuse this candle with the power of the sun God at the height of his reign and command that as it burns, any misfortune and unhappiness we bare will burn away."

The ritual leader places the candle in the cauldron and lights its flame saying "may the power of the sun God above be as the power of the flame below".

The maiden takes the daisy chain from the altar saying "as this daisy chain symbolises the weeds of summer, may it also hold the bad habits, the misfortunes and the wrong doings of our summer. As you take the weeds of summer amongst you, let them hold all that you want banished from your lives."

She spends a moment pushing any of her own banishment requirements into the weed chain and then passes it to the person on her right (so that it will travel around the coveners in a widdershins fashion). As each person takes the weed chain, they too send anything they want banished into it. When the weed chain reaches the maiden again, she holds it up to the sky in the south saying "weeds of summer, weeds of misfortune, weeds of poor judgement, as the summer's zenith passes and the light slowly dies, may our sadness and misfortune die with the fading sun".

She turns and throws the weed chain on the candle flame in the cauldron letting it burn away. As it burns she says "summer fades now, weeds die now, misfortune be gone now. So mote it be!" Everyone says "so mote it be!"

Consecrate and then have the cakes and ale then close the circle. Follow up with a feast.

24th December

What does Christmas mean to a Wiccan?

'Twas the night before Christmas when all through the house, not a creature was stirring, not even a mouse...

So if you're Pagan, Wiccan or a Witch, what will you be doing the night before, and during Christmas? The festive season, embedded in our westernised Christian focused society, is fast approaching and many of us are already preparing for family visits, buying presents and organising our festivities and special celebratory moments. But what does this all mean if you're Wiccan?

That's an interesting question because it raises the ugly notion of how to live through the dominance of a social phenomenon, Christmas, while still remaining true to your spiritual home, Wicca. Personally I don't find it much of a problem anymore but I know many Wiccans do.

For us, we still do all the presents for family, the kids and the grandkids but for friends, I now donate the money I would have spent on their presents to charity and let them know that I love them dearly and in their name have contributed my love and devotion to them to someone in greater need than the both of us.

Without exception, my friends have loved the idea and in fact many of them now do the same thing themselves.

I don't see a problem with giving presents, showing someone you care and that they're special to you and in celebrating the sentiments of family and friendship at this time (or any time) of year. So I make sure that our Midsummer (December is summer for us in Australia) focuses on family, community, sharing and mutual respect and love. We do all the usual Christmas activities but of course I don't follow the spirituality behind it. I do however love the traditions and nuances that makes this time of year so special. At the same time I continue to honour my Gods and Goddesses by making sure I continue to keep them uppermost in my thoughts and don't get swept away by the commerciality that has taken over what Christmas originally meant.

As each of you prepare for the 'silly' season ahead, spare some thought for how you will weld together the spirit of Christmas with your home grown spirituality of Wicca. Take a few moments to consider if you've been seduced by the commerciality, and if the festive traditions you follow reflect the undercurrent of sharing what Christmas should really be about.

31st December

What are your life values?

As a result of someone legitimately asking me to explain the values of CCIWI (www.cciwi.org) this week, it led me to consider what our personal values should be. Other than the obvious Rede and Law of Return, what other, personalised set of values do you hold that reflect the underpinning tenets of Wicca and Paganism in general? What are the set of life principles you hold that guide what you do, how you behave and how you connect with people and the world around you?

A few years ago I was blessed to attend a three day workshop aimed at helping those present identify what their personal values were. As part of the process (which was quite intense and extraordinarily valuable) we each came up with a set of words that articulated the underpinning principles that guided who we were and how we would live our lives. My list had seven words that included creativity, integrity and sincerity. For others, their words included honesty, appreciation, helpfulness, joyfulness, healthy, supportive, and one of my favourites, spiritual. It was an amazing experience that helped each of us to understand ourselves better and have a set of rules that we could check our behaviours against.

Notwithstanding that this time of year many people celebrate New Year, we can also use the end of the calendar year to re-evaluate our life principles and resolve to continue to live our lives according to a set of personal rules that make us better human beings. To that end, I'd encourage you to take a few moments and write down five single words that identify the manner in which you want to live your life from this point forward. What are the words you would want people to describe you with when you pass over and leave this life plane? Would you want to be remembered as joyful? Sincere? Learned? Peaceful? Helpful? What makes you the person you are or aspire to be?

So in conclusion, during the mad rush of the festive season and New Year, gift yourself with some time to write down the five words that describe how you intend to live your Wiccan life from here on in. It may be liberating and enlightening to rediscover your internal, personal life rules so that you're better able to check yourself against them each and every day from here on in. After all, today is the first day of the rest of your life. Make it count.

www.ingramcontent.com/pod-product-compliance
Lightning Source LLC
Chambersburg PA
CBHW031601110426
42742CB00036B/627